BEYOND THE BLACK ROCKS

BELLA MACKENZIE

authorHOUSE®

AuthorHouse™
1663 Liberty Drive
Bloomington, IN 47403
www.authorhouse.com
Phone: 1-800-839-8640

© 2013 by Bella Mackenzie. All rights reserved.

No part of this book may be reproduced, stored in a retrieval system, or transmitted by any means without the written permission of the author.

This is a work of fiction. All of the characters, names, incidents, organizations, and dialogue in this novel are either the products of the author's imagination or are used fictitiously.

Published by AuthorHouse   02/08/2013

ISBN: 978-1-4817-8359-0 (sc)
ISBN: 978-1-4817-8358-3 (e)

Any people depicted in stock imagery provided by Thinkstock are models, and such images are being used for illustrative purposes only.
Certain stock imagery © Thinkstock.

This book is printed on acid-free paper.

Because of the dynamic nature of the Internet, any web addresses or links contained in this book may have changed since publication and may no longer be valid. The views expressed in this work are solely those of the author and do not necessarily reflect the views of the publisher, and the publisher hereby disclaims any responsibility for them.

BRILLIANT SUNSHINE ON the coarse black volcanic sand. Tourists blistering contentedly on their sun beds, too mean to hire parasols to prevent the inevitable sunburn. Still, it was good business for the local hospital. Sandro surveyed the scene with a practised eye. Same scene, day in, day out. Children shrieking happily. Young males drinking steadily. Fathers snoring gently. Mothers anxiously watching their offspring. He glanced hopefully at his watch—another fifty-three minutes and his shift would be over for today. No more idiots to rescue until tomorrow and the next day and the next. He was so tired of scrabbling after stupid holidaymakers on inflatable pink dolphins or green sharks. Despite all the warnings posted everywhere, there was always someone who tried to set sail for the wide Atlantic, blissfully ignorant of the dangerous currents and submerged rocks which lurked only a few hundred metres off shore. Nothing seemed to stop their suicidal urges to drown at sea. Did they leave their brains at home or did the sunshine just addle them?

Sandro was bored. Very bored. Extremely bored. He finally admitted it to himself. He had worked as a lifeguard since he had left school. Five years of parading his tanned muscles on the beach and ogling every fit female in sight. Five years of thinking he had the perfect job. Minimum effort, maximum satisfaction. Outside in the sunshine instead of indoors in some dull college. Just strutting up and down the beach under a cloudless sky. Should be the perfect job. So what had gone wrong? Complacency and laziness had crept in and eroded the satisfaction and now deadly boredom was seeping into any soul he had left. Was this paradise? Was this what he wanted for the next forty or so years?

Suddenly, he understood his sister, Ana. She wanted to get out of the island, out of this narrow-minded community which gossiped its life blood away. She wanted to see the real world, not fester in a so-called 'tourist paradise'. She wanted to make a real contribution to society. While he had wasted his time on the beach and in the bars, chatting up every available female, she had buried her head in her studies and slaved away at her exams. She had all the fire and passion which he, Sandro, lacked. Her exam results were excellent and she had hoped to follow her dream and study Environmental Science on the mainland, perhaps in Barcelona or Madrid. And what was to become of her dream now? All hope of going to university had vanished, just as surely as the fishing business owned by their father. Despite all the hard work, the business was failing, crumbling away, disintegrating like a wet sandcastle. All his Dad's hard graft over the years! All Ana's hard work, endless hours of revision, total commitment and for what?

Something was very wrong in paradise. He must talk to Ana. Inertia had smothered him for too long. She would be pleased he had come to life again and would no doubt tease him mercilessly. He deserved her contempt and her condemnation, but he knew that she would help him too. She would get him back on track and perhaps he could help her, instead of laughing at her dedication and drive. God, what an idiot he was! How short-sighted and stupid!

'Hi! Sandro! A penny for them or even a euro, now that inflation has us in its icy grip,' laughed his English friend, Martin. The relief life-guard lolloped up to him. 'Take it easy, man. You think way too much! Has the sun got to you today?'

Sandro stared at him almost absent-mindedly.

'The trouble is,' he replied 'that I haven't been thinking at all up to now. My brain cells have probably rotted away from lack of use. I've just drifted smugly along, not thinking about anything.'

Sandro looked down at his flip-flops in embarrassment. Abruptly, he changed tack.

'By the way, watch those two idiots with the inflatable over there by the big rock. They won't listen to me about the dangers and the tide is on its way out now. I've rescued them twice today already. I'd like to stick a big nail in their bright pink dolphin before they kill themselves. On the other hand, let them float off into oblivion; it's what they deserve for treating us as their inferiors. I just don't care any more.'

'Hey man! You've got it bad today. Go and have a few beers and shake out of it. Go chat up a bird! You'll feel better for it. Have some fun! See you tomorrow.'

Sandro nodded unhappily, slapped his friend playfully on the back and made his way slowly back up the beach. He glared moodily at his feet, as if they might have some magic answer to his problems. Many a bikini-clad body tried to claim his attention but he was immersed in his own misery. As he reached the recently revamped harbour road (courtesy of the EU), a brand new white minibus screeched to a halt beside him. A familiar figure, the embodiment of their problems at home, shouted a cheery greeting. In no mood for superficial exchanges, Sandro turned on the driver with ill-concealed annoyance and incipient dislike.

'What do you want with me, Uncle Pedro? You creep up behind me in the mornings on my way to work and you are lying in wait for me when I finish my shift. Why?

I've told you so many times I don't want to work for you. I don't want to work with you on your boat. Just leave me in peace. You are making me miserable. In fact, you are making the whole family miserable. You are ruining Dad's business. He's at his wit's end. Mum has had to go to work as a cleaner at that posh new Indian Conference Centre and she hates it. And Ana can't go to Spain now and study as there's no money. So she's moping around. It's all your fault and I hate every bit of it. So just leave me alone!'

Pedro grinned at his naïve nephew. 'Wow! Yer right miserable, aren't yer! Yer have to move with the times, my boy. New equipment, new markets, news ways of operating. Yer Dad is stuck in a rut. And yer Mum? It won't hurt her to do a proper job—her all high and mighty 'cos she's English and bin to university. Why bother educating women? All they need is housework and kids, that's what I say. What's the point in Ana going off to Barcelona? Total waste of time! Her'd be better off looking for a bloke to settle down with and have a few brats to look after.'

Sandro turned away angrily from his Uncle's entrenched prejudices, but Pedro grabbed his arm. 'Yer come in with me, boy, and I'll see yer okay. I'll show yer how to make money and get on.'
Sandro was too choked with conflicting emotions to formulate any sort of reply. Instead, he shook himself

free of his uncle and set off almost at a trot along the cobbled streets towards his home. Why had he not seen through his brutal uncle before? Where had his brains been all these years? Why was Uncle Pedro so bitter and nasty towards his family, yet wanted Sandro to work for him? Never! What right had that hard, unfeeling clod to destroy them? Surprised and shaken by this encounter, Sandro realised that he was at last growing up. Damn Uncle Pedro! For twenty-two long years Sandro had passively accepted everything. What a fool he was! What a spoilt brat! How his family must despise him! Something had to change. And rapidly! Damn! Damn! Damn!

The floor polisher juddered to a halt. Another room finished. Only the Professor's office left to clean. Maria Handez always left his room to last. She instinctively disliked and distrusted the Professor. He would hover smugly around her and make her feel even more humiliated and inferior than she already did. As an English graduate, she could easily have applied for one of the administration jobs in the Centre, but locals were only allowed to fill the menial positions. So, cleaner it was! If only this job would pay for Ana's tuition fees, she would not detest it so much. But it paid only the household bills, which was just as well, as the squid and octopus fishing seemed to be in serious decline. She would have to tolerate this for a lot longer if she were to get Ana away from this chauvinist society. It would all be worth it, if she could just get Ana abroad. She deserved to spread her wings. She would love university. As for her brother, she would dearly love to see Sandro acquire some proper qualifications instead of wasting his time as a glamorous life-guard. Yet he seemed happy. He had no ambition and no desire to improve his lot. What had she done wrong? He was placid, almost passive, with no great interest in anything much except football. Would he ever realise his potential? He was intellectually lazy and nothing seemed to stimulate his imagination, whereas Ana just loved a challenge.

Maria knocked gingerly on the door of the Professor's sanctuary, praying silently that he was still in the lecture theatre or stuffing his face in the dining-room. For once, there was no aggressive bark. The room was deserted. Wonderful! His desk computer was still purring away, flashing messages on the screen. She felt a tremendous urge to delete every email, every last piece of data and cause chaos in this 'Centre of Excellence', where money was squandered on every material luxury imaginable. That new Health and Fitness centre for the delegates! It was amazing, but barely used. They were all too busy eating and drinking and talking drivel over their cocktails. Giving lofty speeches did not seem to influence the environment much. Power point presentations seemed to send most of them to sleep.

It seemed more like a five star holiday camp than a complex to address the issues confronting the planet. Her own daughter, Ana, talked more sense than these delegates ever did. That luxury whirlpool and spa area seemed to eat energy but no-one seemed to object. Oh, what would she give to wrap herself in one of those soft white bath towels after a luxurious spa!

Dream on, thought Maria, as she rammed the plug of the polisher rather viciously into the wall socket. Just get through the shift and keep a roof over their heads. She was lucky to have any job. So many Africans were coming to the island now. They arrived on leaky boats with nothing except the clothes on their backs. They would take any job, no matter how menial. What an awful life they must be escaping from! For some reason, this 'Indian Environmental Centre of Excellence' would not employ any Africans. Security guards kept them well away so as not to disturb their Indian master. They insisted on employing locals from Playa de Santiago to service the Centre—not to do anything vaguely intelligent, of course, just keep it all running smoothly. They wanted to be seen as a 'good' influence on the town, helping to 'reduce their carbon footprint,' whatever that really meant. The locals resented this Indian intrusion into their quiet and uneventful existence but accepted it with an apathy born of fear, tradition and centuries of stagnation. So far, the Centre didn't seem to have done much for the locals. Outsiders had built it; fixtures and fittings had been flown in from the mainland to the small airport, which had been extended to accommodate larger aircraft flying in the rich conference delegates. Uncle Pedro and his pals were raking in the money with their taxi service from the airport to the Centre. Uncle Pedro had bought a new fishing boat equipped with the latest technology and had now cornered the fish market. Uncle Pedro was ruining them. Uncle Pedro was the very encapsulation of evil. How she hated even his name! Uncle Pedro. How she loathed him in person even more!

The floor polisher turned into a machine gun as she massacred Uncle Pedro in her imagination. Damn Uncle Pedro! How two brothers could be so unlike she just could not comprehend. Where Felix was kind and gentle, exciting and full of fun, Pedro was hard as nails and determined to make life thoroughly unpleasant for everyone near him. He had driven any friends away and had many a failed short-lived relationship behind him. He was always moaning about something, even though he was much better off than most of the Islanders. If you were generous, you could call him an entrepreneur, but in reality he just interfered at every opportunity and walked rough-shod over anyone who stood in his way. He also had sticky fingers in a lot of shady deals. Maria despised him with every fibre of her being. Damn Uncle Pedro!

Maria attacked the laminated floor again with her improvised weapon.

'Oh! Professor! You frightened me.'

The small wiry Indian Professor materialised behind her. He did not bother to apologise. Probably didn't know how. He just slammed his puny little fist on the big table by the window and spat out his fury between clenched teeth.

'My secretary has just cleared off back to India because her father has been taken ill apparently. What am I supposed to do? How am I to manage without a secretary? There's a big conference next week on Climate Change and Energy Conservation. It's most inconvenient. And the bitch expects to be paid while she's away. She'll be lucky. This isn't a bloody charity. She can't just disappear when it suits her.'

The Professor collapsed melodramatically into the computer chair, looking as though he might explode again at any moment. Not a shred of compassion for his secretary or her sick father. He really was the embodiment of selfishness, thought Maria. Successfully stifling the desire to strangle him, Maria serenely enquired with a suitable amount of simulated deference:

'Is there no-one else here who can help, Sir?'

'No, there isn't,' he replied coldly, glaring at her with his evil black eyes. Maria struggled with an irresistible impulse to whack the floor polisher into the computer chair and send it and its nasty occupant spinning through the patio doors and out on to the immaculately manicured gardens.

'There's not enough time to get someone in from India and there's no-one local with enough damn brains to do the job properly.'

Swallowing her resentment and disgust at his unnecessary swearing and automatic condemnation of the Islanders, Maria heard herself say:

'My daughter, Ana, is computer literate and extremely organised. She is hoping to study Environmental Science at Barcelona University. She also speaks English fluently. Perhaps she could help you?'

Why on earth had Maria suggested her daughter should come anywhere near this evil little toad? But for the Professor, it would have been a wonderful opportunity for Ana to work here, but to involve her with this self-centred obnoxious specimen of the male race was just not a good idea. Maria blushed furiously and waited for the inevitable dismissive bellow from his Lordship. Instead, she nearly fainted as he snapped back viciously:

'Tell her to come here to me tomorrow at 10.00 and I'll see if she's any damn use.'

Maria retreated hastily with the floor polisher, closing the door quietly behind her. Oh, what had she done? Would Ana cope with that ill-tempered rat? Well, she might. She was strong, was Ana. It would only be for a short while and would be a sort of work experience, though it might put her off men for life! She would be well paid and could save the money for her accommodation at university. Who knows? Perhaps she would be able to follow her dream after all. At least Ana would do something more useful with her education than her mother had done. Maria suddenly realised that this was the first real exchange she had ever had with the Professor and all in English and he had not even realised that she was English and articulate and not just a 'brainless local' as he dismissively called them all. Whew! Maria stowed the polisher out of sight in its cupboard. Retrieving her bag, she made her way quickly towards the exit. Fresh air. Freedom. She felt so vulnerable and insignificant in that place. Now home to sanity.

Pedro sat in the minibus, waiting impatiently for the charter plane. At last he saw it outlined against the rapidly fading light of the evening sky. He watched it circle and eventually land smoothly on the recently extended runway. His greedy little eyes stared intently as the passengers finally disembarked on to the tarmac, while airport staff retrieved the luggage. Soon afterwards the pilot waved and taxied off to the private hangar near the Western perimeter of the airfield. Pedro drove the minibus slowly up to the terminal building and duly loaded up the delegates and their cases. There were hardly ever any Customs checks here as it was an internal flight from Tenerife. No hanging around. This taxi lark was a good money-spinner. The Centre paid him on the dot and the delegates tipped him handsomely. What a doddle!

'Hi Mum! I've laid the table and prepared the salad.'

'Are you feeling okay, Sandro? It's not my birthday until July.'

'Never better!' replied her son, grinning at her. 'Things are going to change around here. I have been a selfish prat. I have let you all spoil me and it hasn't done me any good at all. I'm going to try to put things right.'

'Have you had too much sun today, Sandro?' asked his sister in amazement. 'What's brought all this on?'

'Uncle Pedro ambushed me yet again after work today. He was wheedling and whining. Something inside me just snapped. I suddenly saw him for what he really is. It made me realise that I don't want to work for him or with him or anywhere near him. I don't want anything to do with him. He really gives me the creeps.'

His mother sat down abruptly on the old kitchen chair. 'Not only are my feet killing me, but now my head is, too! I can't take this all in. Is this a permanent conversion or just a temporary state of affairs? You were quite normal when you went to work this morning!'

'I hope it's permanent,' replied Sandro seriously. 'I want to change and do my bit for the family. I've been so selfish and short-sighted. Uncle Pedro has been annoying me for weeks now and it's taken me this long to see through him. I want to find out what is really going on. Why is Uncle Pedro suddenly making so much money and we are struggling? Something doesn't add up. You shouldn't be slaving away as a cleaner, Mum. You're much too good for that. You could manage that Centre standing on your head and they employ you just as a cleaner. It's ridiculous. It's all wrong. And you, Ana, you should be able to go to university. You worked so hard. Who knows, perhaps I'll even go to university as well.'

They were all laughing when Felix entered the kitchen. When he asked what was so amusing, they just laughed even more.

'Sandro has just woken up!' His sister managed to explain at last.

'Did you not go to work today then, boy?' asked his father in alarm. Everyone burst out laughing again, including Sandro, who, for once, was more than happy to be teased. Delighted at the lack of tension in the home, Felix joined in the light-hearted banter and visibly relaxed.

The new fishing boat chugged efficiently out of the harbour into the dark night. Rafa coiled up the ropes while Pedro steered past the jagged rocks out to sea. He was running late as usual and would miss the rendezvous if he wasn't careful. The 'Boss' wouldn't like that and he would get another menacing earful. But he wasn't about to lose this profitable little venture. No way. The 'Boss' might think he was running this organisation, but he was only a small cog in a well-oiled machine. And that machine needed Pedro. If Pedro wasn't there, the whole thing would collapse. Pedro was indispensable. Pedro wasn't going to be blackmailed or frightened by any threats from the so-called 'Boss'.

Having convinced himself that his business venture was secure, Pedro glared again at the luminous dial of his watch and then scanned the angry Atlantic around them. It was getting very choppy. Transfer would be more difficult. Why couldn't they come when the sea was calm? Why should he have to risk his new boat for a load of ungrateful Africans? Another hour passed as they bounced around on the heavy sea. Such a dreary black night. How was he supposed to see anything in this undulating darkness? He must be careful not to run them down inadvertently. No profit in dead bodies.

'Oh, Mum! A job at the Centre for me! You are brilliant!' Ana threw her arms lovingly round her mother's neck.

'Hold on, my girl. It's not all roses up there and it might be a terrible mistake.'

'It is only temporary, Mum. I can cope even if it's horrible. It will be valuable experience for me and I can help pay the bills and I won't feel so guilty any more.'

'Anything you earn, Ana, goes towards your university education. We'll get you to Barcelona somehow. We'll manage here. You're not to worry about that.'

'That is very kind of you Mum, but I must help you and Dad. You have done so much for me.'

'All been worth it, girl', replied her father, giving her a big hug.

'Do I get a hug, Dad, if I go to university too?' Sandro queried playfully.

'You never know your luck, son!'

Laughter erupted around the dinner table again. Then Ana asked worriedly:

'Mum, what is the Professor like?'

Her mother thought for a minute before answering.

'He's an arrogant little weasel with a big ego and no manners. He's smarmy and charming with the delegates and on his best behaviour, because he's getting them to invest in his projects for so-called green energy and conservation projects to save the planet. Personally, I'd like to save the planet from him. He is absolutely horrible to his Indian research team and he is totally vile to the rest of us. We are inferior beings to his way of thinking and deserve nothing. Today was the first time he has ever spoken to me properly. Usually he just barks orders at me like 'do this room later!' or 'get out!' He was so furious today about his secretary having to go and look after her father back in India that he didn't even realise that I, the cleaner, could speak English as well as he could. Nor did he have a shred of sympathy for the family.

Satya, on the other hand, is very kind and caring. He is the Executive Research Co-ordinator and will help you as much as he can. You'll love working with him. I don't know how he stands being treated so badly, but he does. The job he is doing is not what he understood it was going to be and I don't know how long he will tolerate the Professor's ill-tempered outbursts, his laziness and total lack of organisation. They are supposed to be writing a research paper together, but it will be Satya who does all the work and the Professor who claims all the credit.'

'The Professor sounds a real charmer! But he'll meet his match with my sister. Ana will sort out his bad manners.' Sandro grinned cheekily at this sister.

'Thanks for that vote of confidence, young man! At last you recognise my true worth, even if I am but a mere fragile specimen of the female sex!' teased Ana.

'If you can stick it out for a few weeks, Ana, you'll be well paid and it may be useful for your studies,' continued Maria. 'But watch your back and if you are not comfortable up there, then just walk. There's something evil about that selfish little weirdo. He's a real control freak. He certainly freaks me out.'

Sandro stretched out on the old leather sofa beside his sister. Funny, he felt more part of the family now than he ever had. He was so lucky he hadn't blown it completely and ended up on the scrap heap, or in his case, the beach!

Pedro throttled the engine back and scanned the black ocean. Nothing. They had to be somewhere near. Had he come all this way for nothing? Had they changed their minds because of the adverse weather conditions? He circled slowly. It was hard to distinguish anything as they bounced around on the unhelpful waves. Still nothing. He swore violently. Rafa ignored him and kept his comments to himself. Two years of working with his surly employer had taught him that silence was by far the best option.

Pedro swore again. The refugees would all be very sea-sick in this choppy sea when and if he eventually did rendezvous. Did he really want dirty natives vomiting all over his new boat? No, he didn't, but it would be

Rafa cleaning up after them, not him. The howling wind was not helping either. He peered anxiously into the surrounding gloom. Absolutely nothing! Where was that damn boat? Had it sunk in the heavy seas? Then he finally picked out a faint noise to starboard. Voices! At last!

~~~

'Sleep well, Ana! Don't worry about tomorrow. You'll have the Professor eating out of your hand before you know it with that magnetic feminine charm of yours.'

'Thanks, Sandro. I'm so glad you're back with us in spirit. Mum and Dad were worrying about you and what sort of future you would have. We're all so glad you're not going to work for Uncle Pedro. That would have been a betrayal, a total disaster after what he did to our family.'

'I realise that now. I think he sensed that I was getting bored as a lifeguard and he thought I would be an easy target. I very nearly was! What if I hadn't come to my senses? That was a very close call.' Sandro shuddered at the thought.

'But it is still very odd that he wanted to recruit me to work for him, when he has been doing his utmost to destroy Dad's business. I'll have to wake up the few brain cells I have still functioning and see if I can puzzle out what exactly he is trying to achieve. There is definitely something odd going on! Sweet dreams, sis!'

The open boat was not as crowded as he had expected. Perhaps a few had died on the way. It was a long perilous journey from West Africa, with very little food or water and many did not survive. Why did they keep coming? Why come to *his* lovely island? What right had they to stay in La Gomera? What right had these Africans to anything?

As Pedro manoeuvred skilfully alongside, Rafa was ready to arrange the fenders to protect the new fishing boat, his employer's pride and joy.

Pedro growled at Rafa and held up both hands to indicate that ten refugees only were allowed aboard. There was a mad panic as every African tried to scramble desperately on to the life-saving fishing boat. Pedro mercilessly lifted a baseball bat and whacked three sets of hands hard, as the last three refugees tried to hold on to the grab-rail of the boat, pleading to be rescued.

'Okay!' Rafa yelled above the incredible racket of tearful refugees and howling wind. Pedro slammed the engine hard into reverse and distanced himself callously from the flimsy craft. He headed back towards the Island, seemingly unconcerned by the screams from the three Africans left behind. They would probably never make landfall. They were always transferred for the last bit of the journey into leaky rowing boats so as to cover the tracks of the African operators. The system had worked very well so far.

On board, ten pairs of very frightened eyes glinted in the enveloping darkness. Pedro let out a callous, insensitive laugh, as he shifted into a comfortable position for the journey back, the baseball bat ready if necessary. Rafa coiled the ropes up neatly and looked a little warily at their human cargo. He passed a bottle of mineral water to the African nearest him, who accepted with a grateful smile. He gulped the welcome liquid greedily before passing it on to his friend. Then Rafa passed round some biscuits. The Africans relaxed, believing they were now safe and heading for land. Pedro set course for La Rajita, to a small cove on the west coast, accessible only from the sea and therefore unknown to Customs and Excise and anyone else with a bureaucratic axe to grind. This was going to be a long uncomfortable night, unless the wind abated, as the forecast on the radio had promised.

———

Domingo finished the pre-flight checks and obtained clearance for his short flight to Los Rodeos on Tenerife. He taxied along the new runway at the designated speed and into position ready for take-off. Fortunately, the wind had abated considerably. He had already had to while away three long hours in the terminal building waiting for the wind-speed to drop. Safety was paramount for the small charter plane. Fortunately, these adverse weather conditions did not happen too often. He should still be home by midnight and was not on rota again for two days. At least he did not have fretful passengers on this flight, just seven crates of squid in the specially fitted refrigerated section of the luggage hold. Why anyone would want to eat squid was a mystery to him. It was supposed to be a great delicacy and even had aphrodisiac qualities. Maybe he should try some again! Then again, maybe not. He wasn't that desperate to improve his love-life as he didn't actually have one at the moment. Last year his fellow pilot, Chano, had treated him on his birthday to curried squid in the new restaurant on the promenade at Puerto de La Cruz. He thought it was about as tasty as a rubber tennis ball and about as difficult to cut up on a dinner plate. He smiled as he remembered their embarrassment as the squid had suddenly ricocheted off his plate and landed on the floor beside a very elegant lady at the next table. The expression on her face had been priceless and he had found it incredibly difficult to apologise to her for the wayward squid without laughing. The wonderful dessert afterwards and a few beers had also made it quite a memorable evening! Still, each to his own! In these days of recession, if someone wanted seven crates of squid, then he was more than happy to transport it, provided that all the documentation was in order.

The take-off was seamless despite the rather blustery cross-wind. He methodically checked the instruments again as he circled over the airfield and then headed off in a north-easterly direction towards the airport, Los Rodeos in the north of Tenerife, which was used for inter-island traffic and for flights from the Spanish mainland. Sometimes they also used the larger airport of Reina Sofia in the south. At least there were hardly ever any Customs checks for these short charter flights around the archipelago, so there would be no delays when he reached Los Rodeos at 2300 hours.

He could just make out the lights of the harbour in the capital, San Sebastian, far below. It was a pretty island from the air, with its jagged coastline, its vertical cliffs and deep ravines. He would like to explore it one day, if he ever had enough time between flights. Nothing much visible now, of course, in the all-enveloping darkness. Hopefully, he would enjoy some beautiful views on Wednesday, his next daytime trip.

The boat battled on through the heavy sea. The refugees huddled together in the bottom of the boat, hoping this awful journey would end soon. They were cold, exhausted, sea-sick and thoroughly miserable. Thank goodness this fishing boat had rescued them. That small rowing boat had been no match for the rough ocean, which had threatened to engulf them on several occasions. They had been too sick and exhausted to do anything more than hold on grimly to the boat and pray aloud for salvation. Now, they would have a future here on one of the Canary Islands. Back in West Africa a slow death from starvation was always lying in wait. Soon their new life would begin and it would all have been worth it.

At long last the cliffs between La Dama and La Rajita loomed into sight. Fifteen minutes later Pedro throttled back the engine and headed very slowly for the makeshift pier jutting out from the rocks near the cove. Just as well he knew this section of coast so well, for this was not the night to make a navigational error. Too many sharp ledges and barely submerged rocks. He edged the boat forward cautiously until he could come safely alongside the semi-derelict wooden platform, which served as a landing stage for his precious cargo. He put the engine into neutral as Rafa quickly tied up the boat. He flashed the pre-arranged signal into the gloom and received an answer almost immediately. God bless mobile phones, he thought. They function even in really foul weather conditions if you need to organise something like this.

Rafa helped the ten Africans to disembark, albeit somewhat unsteadily. They were almost beyond exhaustion and barely able to stand. Dry land at last! They could scarcely believe it. They mumbled their thanks as Rafa pointed to the sandy cove about three hundred metres away over the huge black rocks. Safe at last!

'Hotel! Hotel!' yelled Rafa above the noise of the wind and waves.

Gratefully, the ten refugees headed off towards the welcoming torchlight. Rafa scurried back on board the trawler, casting off as he went. He hoped the refugees were safe now.

What a night! They were exhausted as they finally motored back unobtrusively into the harbour at Playa de Santiago. That was the most difficult transfer yet. Damned weather! He'd even had to give Rafa the day off. Still, it was easy money really. Much easier than out fishing every day. Pedro laughed to himself. This was real fishing with real bait! All you had to do was to keep your mouth well and truly shut. Rafa knew nothing and wasn't that interested anyway, it seemed. Perhaps he thought he was going to have shares in the business one day. If he ever blabbed, he would find himself with a lead weight round his neck, feeding the sharks lurking offshore. Pedro desperately wanted Sandro as a back-up. He was young; he was bored; he was passive and easily manipulated. By the time he realised what he was involved in, it would be too late. Revenge! Yes, he must get Sandro on board, literally and metaphorically.

'Hey, Sandro! Are you feeling better today?' inquired Martin, as his friend came across the beach to take on the next shift as lifeguard.

'Yes, I'm fine. Sorry about the other day. Any problems here?'

'No, they're all behaving themselves today for a change. Must be a more literate lot who can read the safety signs!'

'What are you going to do now you're off duty?'

'Have a few beers with two of those German girls over there by the rocks and then see how lucky I am.'

'Have fun, then! See you. Don't do anything I wouldn't do!'

'Mum, I'm really nervous. What if he is horrible and I can't do the job?'

'You'll be fine, Ana. He'll be on his best behaviour today chatting you up. Just keep calm and do whatever he asks. If you have a problem, ask Satya. You'll be working in Satya's office, down the corridor from the Professor's room. The Professor insists on his privacy and hardly anyone is allowed into his office. It's his private sanctuary. We often wonder what he does in there that's so secret! Buzz him if you want to talk to him. Whatever you do, don't go knocking on his door. He absolutely hates being disturbed and will throw a real tantrum, as most of the staff have found to their cost.

It will all be a bit strange for the first few days. Starting a new job is always stressful. You will cope, Ana. You are a very competent young lady and I am sure that you will enjoy certain aspects of the job. Just keep your cool when the Professor is around. There are many times when I could have strangled him or attacked him with the floor polisher, because he is so rude and unpleasant, but I have managed to restrain myself! Just! So just stay calm and count to ten slowly. He isn't worth getting upset about.'

'Mum, you should be doing this job, not me. You are far better qualified and more able than I am.'

'Maybe I am,' replied Maria. 'But to the Professor, I'm just a cleaner, the lowest of the low. We locals don't have brains apparently; we're only fit for menial tasks.'

'What a stupid prejudiced oaf!' exclaimed Ana in amazement.

'Ah, well, that's life, darling. You get on now and best of luck. By the way, Sandro asked me to give you this.'

'Chocolates! Wow! He has changed, hasn't he?'

Ana hugged her mother and then set off uphill for the Conference Centre. She decided that she must have at least two chocolates to sustain her for the endurance test ahead. That delicious coffee cream truffle might even calm her nerves!

Far below he could see the impressive cliffs with their welcoming little bays of coarse black sand and clear blue waters. The steep ravines or barrancos, as the locals called them, dissected the island making some areas very isolated and virtually inaccessible. There were the cleverly irrigated terraces laid out on the steep cultivated slopes in the northern half of the island where all sorts of exotic fruit and vegetables could be grown. There was the lush green forest in the centre in the Garajonay National Park and then the strange arid mountainous landscapes to the south. He loved flying over this archipelago: each island had its own special character, but La Gomera with its dramatic landscape was his favourite.

He really must spend a week here getting to know some of the isolated coves and tiny villages perched impossibly in the steep valleys. La Gomera had not been overwhelmed by tourism—yet. It would be great fun exploring using the local bus network and walking. It would make a pleasant change from flying. Perhaps Chano, his fellow pilot, would come with him, if he could tear himself away from his latest girlfriend for a few days. There was a quiet week coming up between conferences when they could perhaps take some time off. He could do with a break. He was beginning to feel that he was glued to the seat of this charter plane and he had no other life at all.

Meanwhile the next few days were going to be really hectic: two trips every morning and afternoon between Tenerife and La Gomera and then on to Lanzarote, transferring delegates to the various venues as required and then returning late to Tenerife with freight. All good for business, this new Indian Centre, but a little too intensive at times. It didn't leave much room for a social life. He rarely saw his fellow pilot, Chano. It would be good to spend some time together and catch up. Chano had a wicked sense of humour and used to keep them all entertained for hours. Those warm lazy evenings drinking beer together in the bars lining the harbour promenade in their temporary home of Puerto de la Cruz on Tenerife seemed but a distant memory. Thinking of that made him thirsty and he resolved to have a couple of chilled beers when he reached home.

'Dad, we need a bit of lateral thinking here. Let's do things differently,' suggested Sandro quietly.

'The fishing isn't paying its way at the moment. We don't know why, but the situation isn't about to change, is it? Supposing instead of fishing, we take tourists out on sight-seeing trips up the west coast to La Dama. We could stop off near one of the little coves for a picnic lunch. I could do a commentary in English. I'm sure I could research some interesting yarns about the various places. We could throw in some whale and dolphin watching. All you would have to do is keep the boat going and not shipwreck us!'

'Cheeky monkey you are!' retorted his father. 'I've been sailing these waters for forty odd years, so I think I'll just about manage to navigate us safely there and back!'

'I hope so! What do you think, Dad?'

'Well, it's a good idea. As you say, for some reason the actual fishing is a waste of time at the moment. I don't know where all the squid have gone. The experts say that squid breed quickly and therefore they are a remarkably sustainable food source. We have never over-fished them, but they have just disappeared from my usual fishing grounds and I am at a loss to understand it.'

'Yes, there's something very fishy about that!' said Sandro, laughing. 'Perhaps Uncle Pedro is going out in his boat at night and catching every squid in sight! Perhaps he is charming them away to a new habitat! We'll get to the bottom of that little mystery one day but meanwhile you've got to make a living.'

'Yes, indeed. The idea sounds great, but when exactly could *you* do these trips?'

'On my days off,' came the prompt reply. 'I have a lot of holiday owing to me as well. If the tourist idea is successful, we could even expand and run sport fishing trips for moray eel or octopus for the tourists as well. I'll give up my job as a lifeguard and come in with you full-time and see if we can't get this business moving again.'

'But you never wanted to come in with me into the business,' replied Felix in amazement. 'You said you hated fishing and boats and the sea and me, too, if I remember correctly!'

'Sorry about that, Dad! I think I might just have grown up a bit since then. I'm really serious about this. I'm not going to let all your hard work go down the drain. I'm not going to let you worry yourself sick about going bankrupt and losing everything. And I am definitely not going to let Uncle Pedro defeat us.'

'Good Heavens! You really have woken up, my son. Okay, okay, let's try it. Let's go for it, partner!'

They hugged and set off down to the harbour together, laughing companionably.

Ana went through all the surprisingly elaborate security checks for her new job at the Conference Centre and then followed the directions given to Satya's office.

'Hello, Ana! Very pleased to meet you. Your Mother is always talking about you.'

'Hello, Satya. Mum is always talking about you, too, so I am very pleased to meet you.'

'You'll be working here in my office, so if you need any help at all, just ask.'

'Thank you so much, Satya. I am really nervous. I hope I don't annoy the Professor.'

'That wouldn't be difficult. He is often on a rather short fuse, so be warned and keep your distance if you can. I don't quite know why he is so uptight at the moment. The research projects are all going quite well, the Centre is making pots of money for him, so I really don't understand why he is so short-tempered all the time. Don't take any of it personally. Just keep your cool and you will be fine. By the way, he has been delayed and won't be here until 11 o'clock so I'll show you around, shall I?'

'Yes, please. That would be great. All I know at the moment is the cupboard where the floor polisher lives!'

'I'm not sure that will help you much with all the emailing and photocopying you will have to do!' Satya smiled and reflected that Ana was a real credit to her Mum and it was going to be great fun working with such a vibrant and attractive young lady. He hoped that she was not too sensitive and could just ignore any temper tantrums emanating from the unpredictable Professor and not become upset.

―❦―

Five hours later Sandro and Felix returned home, having given the boat a spring-clean, ready for its new role as tourist attraction. Excitedly, they told Maria their plans and what they had achieved so far. She was delighted, all the more so because father and son were obviously getting on so well together and Sandro seemed really animated and more committed than she had ever seen him. Who would have thought that five hours cleaning up a fishing vessel could have been so inspiring! Long may this newly discovered peace and happiness continue! She had been so worried this morning about Ana working with the Professor that she had got very little done. Now she set to with renewed energy. She would hear from Satya later on how Ana had managed, as he was working late tonight.

―❦―

In a bar down by the harbour Martin and Sandro were enjoying a beer together. 'Can you teach me how to whistle, Sandro?'

'So that the girls come running, you mean, Martin!'

'No, you idiot! That special whistling they use on this island.'

'Oh, that,' replied Sandro somewhat dismissively. 'We had to learn all that at school. The government made it compulsory as part of our so-called cultural heritage. I've never actually used it except when we were messing about at school.'

'What's it for, then?'

'It's called Silbo Gomero. It's a sort of whistled language, used by the original inhabitants, the Guanches, who apparently came across from Africa. All these deep ravines we have here on La Gomera make getting around and communication very difficult, so they developed this long-range whistling to talk to each other. Otherwise, you'd have to climb up to the top of each steep valley and then scramble down the other side to talk to your neighbours. I expect you'd have forgotten what you wanted to say by the time you'd done that!'

'That's fascinating,' said Martin. 'I expect the whistle language is quite useful for emergencies. Can you teach me some?'

'Okay! So long as you promise not to use it on the girls round here!'

'Deal! I'll get you another beer.'

'Ana is lovely and she coped very well. We didn't have any bad tempered outbursts today from His Lordship, so all was peaceful. I hope she wants to stay. She certainly brightens the place up!'

'Oh, thank goodness, Satya. I was so worried. I don't know what I was thinking of when I suggested Ana for the job. I wouldn't wish that little weasel on anyone. I really don't know how you have endured it all for so long.'

'Stop worrying, Maria. You have a daughter to be proud of and she'll be more than a match for the Professor once she has settled in! She has a great sense of humour and we shall get on famously together. It is rather a baptism of fire for her at the moment with this big conference looming, but I'm sure she will cope with everything flung at her.'

'Thank you so much, Satya, for taking her under your wing. Ana is a hard worker and very meticulous. I would really like to see her follow her dream and read Environmental Science at Barcelona. She studied so hard for all her exams and was really committed to getting the highest grades possible, so that she could make the world a better place. Youthful idealism, I know, but she does want to try to make a difference and I will encourage her all I can.'

Maria perched on the edge of Satya's desk and said rather wearily:

'I have had such a strange day today, Satya. First of all, I was really unsettled about Ana; I did hardly any housework and what I did do, I had to do over again as my mind wasn't on it. Then Felix and Sandro came home, best buddies, having spent five happy hours together down at the harbour, cleaning up the boat. Five hours working together and they were still laughing when they got home. That was quite a shock, a very pleasant one, but a shock nevertheless. Then they both told me they are going to do charter trips along the coast for the tourists. That's why they had spring-cleaned the boat. AND they are considering going into partnership together, if the venture is successful. I can't believe it. I just can't. Sandro was always dead against going into the business, much to my husband's annoyance. Instead he went into a dead-end job as a lifeguard to avoid both the business and going to college, much to *my* annoyance! He never bothered much with his studies. He couldn't wait to go surfing with his mates or play football. Any activity to avoid schoolwork. It was a constant battle to persuade him to complete his homework every day. He never seemed interested in anything except sport and now he seems a reformed character. I have so many conflicting emotions that I am quite exhausted. My world is a bit topsy-turvy today and I am a bit wary of what might happen next!'

'You are working far too hard and worrying too much, Maria. Relax and enjoy yourself more. Everything will work out in the end. In any case, we can't change what happens. We can't change fate.'

'I expect you're right, Satya. I'll try. I suppose I'd better get on with the cleaning or I won't get it all done in time and there will be ructions. Thank you again, Satya, for all the translation work. I love doing it and it helps so much with all the bills. See you tomorrow!'

'Dad, what do you think of this design?' asked Sandro, handing over a leaflet about their proposed charter trips.

'I've just printed this off. I can change it any way you want. We could go up the west coast two days a week and go up the east coast two days a week. We could do weekend or evening sport fishing trips, if there were any demand. I bumped into Rafa on the way back up from the beach this morning. We got chatting and I told him what we were trying to do and he very kindly said we can have four heavy duty sport fishing rods and reels that they aren't using any more. The tourists could have a lot of fun wrestling a moray eel out of the water, couldn't they?'

'Yes, they certainly could. Those moray eels are really aggressive. They even have two sets of jaws to clamp their prey, before they rip the flesh off. I remember vividly the first one I ever caught. It was so strong that it nearly dragged me into the sea with it. Grandpa had to haul me back in by my ankles and teach me how to play the fish properly. It was frightening but great fun. Those eels fight really hard and I'm sure the tourists would love the experience. Doesn't Uncle Pedro need the rods?'

'Apparently not. Rafa said they had been in the shed for ages and Uncle had forgotten all about them.

They don't use them now. His comments about Uncle Pedro are not repeatable.'

'Pedro isn't popular with Rafa then either!'

'Not from what he said! I think Rafa would work for someone else if only he could. He said he was very glad that I wasn't going to work for my uncle. So am I! I can't believe I even considered it. I must have been half asleep. What about the flier, then, Dad? Do you want anything changed or are you happy with it?'

'It's very good. That should get us started. We will have to adapt it, if necessary, when we see what proves popular and what falls flat. Would you like to print some off and I'll help you distribute them? You've done well, Sandro. Thank you.'

Another beautiful day as he touched down at La Gomera airport. This DHC-6 Twin Otter was a joy to fly. It was dependable and very versatile, ideal for island-hopping. With its two powerful engines he could see why it was so popular with pilots. It was a first class utility aircraft. Both he and Chano enjoyed flying it and it made all their assignments so much easier.

He taxied to within thirty yards of the terminal building as requested and came to a smooth standstill. The fourteen passengers stretched and blinked as the bright sunlight flooded in through the now open cabin door. They disembarked in a very orderly fashion and made their way into the terminal building to wait for their luggage and then the minibus. The following wind meant that they had arrived somewhat ahead of schedule, but no matter. Domingo taxied off to the hangar at the far end of the airfield. He had eight hours before his return flight and he had decided to spend the day exploring some of the island. He picked up his rucksack, locked up the plane and walked back to catch the local bus to the Garajonay National Park Visitors' Centre. The Park had been declared a World Heritage Site in 1986 by UNESCO and he was curious to see this special ecosystem and ancient laurel forest. He had brought his waterproofs, as recommended by the guide book. Apparently you could get absolutely soaked at this time of year in the forest with the condensing mist. That's what made the forest so luxuriant, as well as the numerous springs and streams in the area. He was looking forward to trekking through some of it. He broke into a run and just made it to the bus. He settled back in his seat to enjoy the scenic trip.

'I am absolutely shattered, Satya. I have never crammed so much into one day in my life! All those lecture notes to type and photocopy and collate. And then the Professor changed his mind twice and I had to retype two lots for him about 'interdisciplinary academic fields' and 'integrated, quantitative approaches for improving environmental quality' and 'polycentric innovation and expertise.' It is all quite interesting, but it does seem incredibly vague. I shall have to take a copy home and study it and work out what this 'complex evaluation of alternative systems' is all about.'

'You have done very well, Ana. Don't worry too much about all the environmental waffle! Just curl up on the settee tonight and have a large glass of wine and relax. Tomorrow will probably be even more hectic and I suspect he may change his lecture topics yet again. So be prepared!'

'Oh dear, is he always so disorganised?'

'I'm afraid so! But don't let it worry you. That's why he has us minions running around after him! He is actually quite an inspiring lecturer and all the academics speak very highly of him. He is always super charming when he has a paying audience.'

He paused, seeing Ana's worried expression and asked what was wrong.

'Nothing serious, Satya. It's just all these emails that I haven't sorted through yet. I've just been so busy typing and photocopying and collating that I haven't got round to them. Do you think it would be okay if I downloaded them on to my computer at home? I want to check through everything and make sure I don't miss anything. I haven't really had enough time here without interruptions to do any of it properly and they might be crucial for the conference next week, for all I know. When I skimmed through, there were several which were totally incomprehensible so I'd like some peace and quiet to go through them.'

'I'm sure that will be fine. Just don't tell anyone. Security and all that Health and Safety rubbish you know. The Professor takes that all incredibly seriously and treats all the information in the Centre as though it were a state secret. Nothing, absolutely nothing leaves this building under any circumstances according to him! Heaven help anyone who disobeys this edict!'

Ana laughed at Satya's excellent impression of the Professor holding forth.

'Okay. Message received loud and clear! Downloading emails now and we haven't had this conversation!'

'No worries. Just don't spend too much time wading through them. You're entitled to time off. We need you bright-eyed and bushy-tailed tomorrow morning.'

'I won't,' promised Ana. 'I really love working here with you, Satya. I never realised admin work could be such fun.'

'It is actually very dull and dreary, but if you didn't laugh, you would go slowly mad. I think your dry sense of humour has rescued me from incipient insanity.'

'I'm glad of that!' replied Ana, grinning.

The bus climbed tortuously up the steep valley towards the National Park. Strange rock formations appeared in the distance: 'chimneys of basalt left over from the eroded extinct volcanoes' according to the guide book. It looked like a weird film-set for some prehistoric landscape. Hopefully there weren't any dinosaurs roaming around in heavy disguise! The bus slowed and halted by the entrance to the Park. Domingo gathered up his map and rucksack and stepped down from the bus. He double-checked the departure times with the driver. He could not afford to be late back to the airport.

What a strange place! It was a sort of tropical rain-forest atmosphere with twisted trunks of laurel trees and straggly ferns wrapping themselves amorously around his walking boots. He hoped that the map was accurate and he did not disappear without trace in this peculiar primeval landscape which seemed almost impenetrable in parts. The highest point was apparently 1487m, but he would not manage that today with his restricted schedule. He headed off in that general direction and eventually came out on to a sort of plateau which was covered in thick moss and heather. The view was amazing. He could see two of the other Canary Islands quite clearly and recognised them as La Palma and El Hierro. He could also just make out the slopes of the dormant volcano Mount Teide swathed in cloud on Tenerife.

He walked on further, admiring the steep escarpments below him which he had seen so many times when flying overhead. It was eerily quiet. No birds singing; in fact, no birds. There seemed to be a huge network of footpaths here with very few signposts, so he must be careful. It was very humid in this sub-tropical forest and the guide book was accurate about getting wet. He came across the wooden statues of Gara and Jonay, the doomed Guanche lovers mentioned in the guide book. The tale was a bit like Romeo and Juliet. She was a princess from La Gomera and he was a King from one of the provinces in Tenerife. At the engagement party on La Gomera, the volcano, Mount Teide on Tenerife, had erupted. This was taken to be a bad omen so the wedding was immediately cancelled. Jonay was forced to return to Tenerife but he was so miserable without his true love that one night he swam across to La Gomera to rejoin his beloved. Both families were furious and pursued the lovers relentlessly. Trapped on the mountain, they decided to die together. Suicide was apparently an honourable option in those days!

Enough romance for one day. He must make his way back to the bus for the airport or he would find himself unemployed in the very near future and that would be decidedly unromantic.

When Maria came home, she found Ana curled up on the settee, muttering indistinctly in her sleep. She sat down quietly in the armchair opposite and picked up the translation work she was doing. Eventually, Ana stirred and opened her eyes.

'Welcome back, Ana! You look very tired. Is the job awful?'

'I am tired Mum, but the job is okay. It is really smashing being in the same office as Satya. He has managed to stop me from making any horrendous mistakes. I've just been so busy audio-typing lecture notes for the Professor. If I have to type 'interdisciplinary' or 'multidisciplinary' one more time, I think I'll crack up! I don't see much of the Professor. He just leaves piles of work on my desk with instructions on post-it notes everywhere and I put what I've completed in the tray outside his office. He hasn't said a word to me. He hasn't even commented on the work I've done, so I presume it was all accurate. He was in his office this morning shouting and swearing about something or other, but we just kept a very low profile. Satya tells me that he has become quite adept at that! It's quite a laugh really.'

'I'm glad you can see the funny side, Ana. Things will quieten down when the conference is over next week. It won't be so stressful then.'

'Do you think the Professor will just get rid of me once the conference is over?'

'Satya thinks not. The other lady will be in India for at least five weeks, as her father is very ill and she is an only child. Poor thing! We don't even know if she will get her job back. She ought to, of course, but the Professor runs the show there and is a law unto himself. We assume that he owns the Centre and is answerable to no-one else, but we don't really know what his status is. Perhaps there are other shareholders or a consortium owns it and he is given a free hand in running it. He is a very big fish in the academic world and seems to attract lots of sponsorship and investment, which is very good for business. No-one really knows much about any of it but I suppose that while it's all profitable, no-one really cares.'

'You're getting cynical in your old age, Mum! How about a large glass of wine each? I reckon we deserve it, don't you?'

Ten days later at Los Rodeos Airport, North Tenerife, just before dawn . . . .

Under cover of darkness the courier drove slowly up to the charter plane hangar. The headlights were switched off so he had to rely on the moonlight. He stopped the engine and listened intently. Then he opened the door to the hangar with his duplicate key and unloaded the crates from his truck, placing them carefully beside the specially adapted cargo bay of the DHC-6. Job done! He locked up the hangar carefully and climbed back into the truck. He drove unobtrusively around the perimeter of the airfield until he came to the main gate which opened electronically with his gadget and closed silently behind him as he vanished into the deserted countryside. Back home for a well-earned rest!

'That was the busiest fortnight of my life, Satya. Do you think the Professor will give me my notice when he comes back from Lanzarote? Perhaps he doesn't need me now that the conference is over?'

'Oh, he'll still need you, Ana. Nothing is ever quiet here for long! You did very well to survive under so much pressure, so you deserve a quiet spell to catch up. He has been surprisingly well-behaved since you arrived. You must radiate some magic chemical that calms him down! So, please don't go!'

'Oh, I don't want to go. I love working here with you. Oh Satya! I'm so sorry! I've been so busy with all this typing and photocopying that I haven't asked what *you* are actually researching.'

'I'm not sure myself anymore! I thought I was co-ordinating the research on the biological diversity of the areas which have experienced some environmental degradation. But the Professor has a nasty habit of redefining the terms of reference, so I don't really know what exactly we are writing this research paper on. I was becoming so frustrated that I decided to take the initiative and co-ordinate various on-going projects in the archipelago, which I think will prove of interest and then filter out what he might want afterwards. There is some really interesting research going on around the western margins of the Garajonay Forest, where they are trying to rescue some of the species of native plants like mosses and lichens which are on the international list as critically endangered. It's a fascinating ecosystem there. This in turn is being linked to global climate change studies and then to further evaluation of the role of airborne contaminants in the environmental degradation. Then that is linked to another on-going project about natural resource management with particular regard to the giant lizards on La Gomera.

It really is far too wide-ranging a topic area and I'm not sure where it is all going and what it has to do with the 'Multidisciplinary Policies and Integrated Approach' which the Professor rattles on about. No doubt all will become crystal clear one day.'
'I'll make you a large cup of strong black coffee, Satya, and you must have some of Mum's delicious chocolate cake. That should help you see more clearly! I can't have you worrying about enormous lizards and air pollution at this time of the day! That's much too problematical!'

'That would be most welcome, Ana. Please thank your Mum for me. Her cake always makes all my problems disappear!'

The pristine ex-fishing boat chugged happily into the harbour and moored alongside the quay. Sandro helped the tourists to disembark and gratefully accepted their generous tips. When they were out of earshot, Sandro almost shrieked with joy.

'We've done it, Dad! It's a success! Even though the island is actually not over busy at the moment we have still had a full boatload every day and we're fully booked for the next three weeks as well.'

Felix hugged his son, a mixture of relief and pride on his face. It was a very successful business venture so far, but they must be cautious. He didn't want any over-optimistic chicken-counting.

'You have done brilliantly, son. Your commentary is fascinating. I'd forgotten that story about Gara and Jonay. The tourists loved that one. Holiday romance, eh! And all that information about squid, dolphins and pilot whales. I never realised you knew so much about marine life!'

'I don't really. I just looked it all up! It was amazing when those dolphins came over and played around the boat, wasn't it? The tourists loved it. They were a wonderful sight. The dolphins seem to appear on cue every time we go there. They must recognise the boat and like the bits of mackerel I give them! I haven't been up that stretch of coast near La Dama for years. You used to take us to the little coves near there for picnics when we were nippers, didn't you? I'd forgotten how very wild and rocky it was. I'm glad you're reasonable at navigation, Dad!'

'I'm not too old to clip your ears, young man.'

'True,' replied Sandro, 'but you need me now as tourist guide and I'd put everyone off if my ears were lopsided or even cauliflowered!'

Grinning at each other like proverbial Cheshire cats, they made the boat secure for the night, climbed on to the quay and headed contentedly for home.

'Ana, would you fancy some experience of environmental research on Saturday, if you're not busy?' Satya looked up from his laptop and smiled.

'Is that the scientific equivalent of 'would you like to come upstairs and see my etchings,' Satya?'

Satya laughed so much that she thought he would do himself a mischief. Eventually, he managed to splutter:

'No, not really! Honestly! I need to go to Garajonay to collect some research data and then I thought we might go down to the cliffs where the lizards are supposed to live. They are quite elusive, but I thought it would be an enjoyable outing.'

'That would be lovely. I'll bring a picnic, shall I?'

'No, no, don't do that. I would like to take you out to lunch in a local restaurant and you can teach me about the local specialities. It's no fun eating out on one's own and I haven't had the courage to try many of the Spanish dishes yet. I just don't understand the menus and I like to know what I'm eating!'

'Okay, it's a deal! I'm sure I can find some delicious food for you to try. How do you fancy curried squid in octopus sauce?'

Satya started laughing again, as Ana winked at him conspiratorially. Just as well the Professor was away. The atmosphere in the Centre was totally different!

Chano checked the information on the manifest against the crates in the hold and secured them meticulously. He did the usual visual pre-flight checks and then climbed into the pilot's seat. Ten minutes later he left the hangar area and taxied down slowly to the terminal building to wait for his six passengers. The airport staff loaded the luggage and helped the passengers into the plane. None of them looked very well. Perhaps early mornings didn't agree with them. Chano ensured that their seatbelts were fastened and went through the safety routine with them. He waited for clearance from air traffic control. Ten minutes later, they were circling over the airport after a smooth take-off. Clear skies with some high wispy fair weather cloud. Easy hop today across to La Gomera, with fine weather forecast so very low risk of turbulence. Just as well because the two passengers nearest him looked distinctly unwell. Must have been quite a night out! He hoped they wouldn't be sick on the way over. He really didn't want to spend his free time cleaning up vomit on the plane. He hoped to take the bus into town and relax for a while between flights.

The door opened as Maria arrived with the floor polisher. She was pleased to see Satya was still working.

'Hi Satya! I was hoping to catch you and thank you again for all the translation work you have passed on to me. It's a bit more inspiring than cleaning offices!'

'You're very welcome, Maria. You should be employed on some wonderful research project, not charging around with a mop and duster. Your intelligence is being wasted. By the way, I've asked Ana to help me with a project on Saturday near Garajonay. Is that okay with you?'

'Of course it is, Satya. You don't need my permission. Ana is nineteen now and well able to decide for herself.'

'I wanted to make sure you had no objections. I value our friendship.'

'And I, yours! I hope you both have a lovely day.'

'Thank you, Maria. Your daughter has threatened me with curried squid in octopus sauce when I take her out to lunch.'

'Enjoy it! There is absolutely nothing quite like curried squid! It could be a life-changing experience! Anyway, I'd better get on with the cleaning now or I'll be out of a job!'

'You'll be pleased to know that the coast is clear. His Lordship has been delayed and won't be back from Lanzarote until tomorrow. I expect he'll be in a foul mood then.'

'You've just made my day, Satya. Don't work too late, will you! You don't want to be too tired to enjoy your squid on Saturday!'

'Dad, you're good at puzzles, aren't you? I've got all these coded emails from work that I can't make head or tail of. I don't know if they are important or not. Could you have a look for me, please?'

Felix came over to the computer and stared rather warily at the screen.

'Yes, of course I will. Could you print them out for me, Ana? It hurts my eyes looking at that screen. I'm really not into these new-fangled contraptions.'

Ana duly printed them off and her father settled down in the armchair with a notepad and pen and concentrated on the emails. Ana quietly worked her way through some more irrelevant emails, when an unusual one attracted her attention. It was from an Indian girl called Tamarai pleading for information about her father, Karthik. They had not heard from him for a long time and were getting worried that something had happened to him. Ana emailed her back, asking her for more information and saying she would do her best to help her. She asked Tamarai to use Ana's personal address and not that of the Centre. Obviously the Professor had seen the emails and chosen not to answer them. Ana knew how she would feel if her Dad disappeared, so she wanted to help the Indian girl if she could. She trolled through more emails and found several more from Tamarai, who was obviously growing increasingly desperate for information. Poor girl! Her whole family must be so miserable and upset.

The courier arrived at the airport and took charge of the crates which Chano had flown from Tenerife. The surly Pedro had collected his six passengers and headed off to the hotel. He didn't care for Pedro. He felt uneasy when he was around and he really had no idea why. Still, they had very little to do with each other, so his feelings were rather irrelevant. Chano shrugged. He had four hours before his next flight and fortunately none of the passengers had been sick in the plane, though they had looked pretty green at times. Two of them were so weak that he had had to call for help to take them off the plane and get them across to the minibus. They were lucky that it had been such a straightforward trip. He locked up the plane and walked back down to the terminal to catch the bus into town. He could spend some time down by the harbour, watching the boats come in and out. There was sure to be someone to talk to.

It was rather overcast as Ana and Satya set off for Garajonay. Satya was in high spirits but drove the Conference Centre Jeep carefully along the winding road which climbed steeply to the head of the ravine. He glanced sideways at Ana, who seemed relaxed and happy. He had been looking forward to this all week. The cloud was gradually dispersing as they reached Chipude at approximately 1100metres on the western edge of the Garajonay forest. He turned left into a rough track and stopped the car.

'We shall have to walk the last bit, Ana. The research hut is down this track and Jeevan has left the documents for me in the safe.'

Satya pointed out some of the flora a few metres to the side of the track. He told her the botanical and English names of the various shrubs and trees and explained about their preferred habitat and characteristics. Ana listened avidly and the time passed quickly. Satya duly retrieved the study data that his colleague had left for him and they then made their way slowly back to the car.

They carried on westwards towards the coast and stopped several times to admire the lush palm groves and terraced slopes of the valleys. They pulled into a lay-by near some very steep cliffs.

'Lizard country!' said Satya dramatically. 'Our chances of seeing one are remote in the extreme, but we can have fun looking, can't we?'

'Tell me about these big lizards. We only see little ones at home. Mum is terrified of them and any other creature with more than two legs. If we hear a scream, we know there is a spider or beetle in the kitchen and Mum needs our help urgently! Mum is very practical and down to earth, but any creepy-crawlies really freak her out.'

'I must remember that and make sure I evict any livestock before your Mum comes to the office! I don't want her screaming in there. It might be totally misconstrued!'

Ana was still laughing as Satya continued.

'Anyway, you wanted to know about the lizards. Well, they arrived from Africa about fifteen million years ago and seemed to be around until the early nineteen hundreds. After that there were no live sightings and it was feared that this giant lizard species was extinct. Then in March 2000 two Spanish scientists came across six of them living near here on the cliffs. Everyone was very excited and a programme was set up to monitor them at regular intervals. The lizards can apparently grow up to forty centimetres in length but you'll be pleased to know that they are herbivorous, so no threat to us! Unfortunately for the lizards, they are very slow movers and are easily caught by the wild cats round here. They are now protected by international law (not that the cats know that) and a captive breeding programme was set up some time ago to try to ensure preservation of the species and hopefully to increase the number of lizards on the island. They tend to live near the most inaccessible ledges and crevices in these very steep sun-baked cliffs, so I don't think we shall see any, unless they happen to be out sunbathing. Personally, I have no head for heights and rock-climbing is definitely not my thing, so we'll just admire the view, shall we?'

Maria could hear the Professor shouting on the phone, verbally exploding with rage by the sound of it. She couldn't help overhearing snatches of the odd one-sided conversation as she dusted the shelves in the corridor. She knew she ought not to listen but curiosity got the better of her. Something was 'utterly stupid' and 'totally brainless.' Someone should 'take them back to 'Karthik.' 'They' should 'get on with it.'

The Professor was almost screaming with fury now that it was definitely not his problem and not to contact him about it again under any circumstances. Maria deemed it would be a matter of prudence and self-preservation to disappear rapidly down the hall into another office. What a strange conversation! Who on earth were 'they'? Where was 'Karthik?' It certainly wasn't anywhere on La Gomera. It sounded vaguely Scandinavian.

<hr>

'Right, Ana. Please tell me what all these weird items are on the menu. I don't recognise any of them and I'm not very adventurous. You choose something for me.'

'Okay. Let's see! First of all we'll have *potaje*. That's a really thick soup, almost a stew, with lots of vegetables in. Then we'll have some fish, not squid, you'll be pleased to hear. I think we'll try *caballa con salsa mojo picante*. That's fried mackerel with a spicy pepper sauce. And we'll have special wrinkly potatoes which we call *papas arrugadas*. They are boiled in their skins in sea-water and are absolutely delicious. For the dessert, there is *papaya con miel de palma*. That's papaya fruit with honey from the palm tree, similar to maple syrup or you could have *quesillo*, which is a lovely baked cheese cake. How does all that sound?'

'Splendid! Would you be kind enough to order it, please? We might end up with something totally different if I try to pronounce that lot in Spanish!'

'Of course I will. Your English is perfect, Satya. You can't expect to speak fluent Spanish, too!'

'I was trying to learn some basic Spanish, but I rather lost interest when the research projects kept being altered and the Professor became so thoroughly obnoxious. He ridicules people in public, which is extremely humiliating, both for the victim and the unfortunate audience. Most of us have been at the receiving end of that tactic. The other day he ranted and raved at my colleagues, Amit, Sadiq and Jeevan in the corridor over something quite trivial. It was really embarrassing for all concerned. Even worse is his attitude to the local staff, like your Mum. He treats them very badly indeed and yet they all work so hard and keep the Centre running very efficiently. He doesn't appreciate them at all. He's always having a go at the security team about confidentiality and double-checking everyone's credentials and every bag. Does he expect terrorists to inveigle their way into this Environmental Centre? He is totally paranoid and we have absolutely no idea why.'

'I can't say I really appreciate having my handbag checked so rigorously every day,' interjected Ana. 'I suppose it is necessary and I just have to accept it. The security guards always grin when they see what I have in my handbag. Sandro always teases me that I always carry 'everything except the kitchen sink' in it! Yesterday my bag bulged more than usual and the guards were joking about me having a hammer in there as well! They're a cheeky lot but very friendly. I'm almost tempted to put a hammer in my handbag tomorrow in order to see their reaction!'

'That would certainly be quite interesting. You would probably set off a major security alert and be banned for ever, so please don't! Somehow the security precautions all seem so pointless. We're researching the biodiversity of the Islands, the flora and fauna, not nuclear weapons.'

Satya paused in his diatribe and said reflectively: 'The other aspect I find very disturbing is that the Professor is certainly a brilliant lecturer on his subject, but deep down he doesn't really seem to care about the real issues concerning the Centre. That's what we all find so frustrating and irritating. His mind always seems elsewhere and you can't pin him down to any practical application of all the research. So Amit, Sadiq, Jeevan and I are just developing our own projects at the moment and keeping a safe distance. We are all rather disillusioned. In fact, I was so fed up that I was seriously considering leaving when you suddenly came to work at the Centre. Now I look forward to every day. You are so easy to talk to. You have cheered me up immensely with your youthful enthusiasm and idealistic values and I'm very grateful.'

'I'm so grateful you are there, Satya. You have helped me so much and made a repetitive job interesting and amusing. I don't think I would have coped without you. I ought to be treating you to lunch, not the other way round!'

The waiter arrived with two large steaming bowls of *potaje* and a generous supply of local bread. 'It smells absolutely wonderful!' said Satya, 'and not a squid in sight!'

Sitting comfortably in the battered old armchair opposite his wife, Felix had a Eureka moment and almost shouted in his excitement.

'Hey, Maria, I've just cracked the email code! It's taken me nearly two hours but I've really enjoyed doing it. It's certainly a very complicated one.'

'Well done, Felix. Ana will be delighted.'

'I'm not so sure she will. I don't think any of this is going to be of much interest to Ana. It has nothing whatsoever to do with environmental research, as far as I can see. It's all medical stuff about procedures for patients with 'nephropathy' amongst other conditions. Have you any idea what that might be, Maria?'

'No, sorry, darling, not a clue, but I could look it up for you, if you'd like. Definitely sounds more medical than environmental. Probably Satya will know more about these emails. Perhaps it's some research sent to the Professor for peer review. Anyway, I'm sure Ana will be very relieved that you have puzzled it all out for her.

I know she was worried that she had missed something. She's a perfectionist.'

'So am I! I'm just not very good at it!' laughed Felix. 'I'll transcribe it all for her and she can see if any of it is relevant.'

'How about a glass of chilled wine to celebrate the great breakthrough?'

'Good idea, Maria!' Felix stood up, stretched and wandered over to the kitchen to fetch two glasses from the cupboard near the larder.

'Red or white, Maria, or green with yellow spots?'

'White, please. One day, Felix, I'll call your bluff and you'll have great difficulty in finding green wine with yellow spots, when I ask for it!' replied Maria, sighing contentedly. 'I do hope that Ana and Satya are having a lovely day. They seem to get on really well together and he is quite protective towards her. I thought I had made a terrible mistake with a job at the Centre for her, but so far, so good. She has threatened Satya with squid in octopus sauce for lunch. She said he ought to try some of the more unusual cuisine that the Canary Islands have to offer.'

'Well done, Ana! Satya sounds very nice. I'm looking forward to meeting him. He's welcome to the squid and the octopus. I'd rather have your wonderful home cooking any day, Maria, than some of these so-called delicacies in weird and wonderful sauces!'

Chano had been wandering quietly around the harbour for about ten minutes when he came across one of the fishermen, who was packing his catch in crates with ice. Chano found out he was called Rafa and he chatted to him about the fish and was fascinated to learn it was squid, as he had never seen the whole fish before, only the bits of curried squid which he and Domingo had attacked in the restaurant that time last year. He didn't think it looked anymore appetizing now than it did then. He explained to Rafa that he was one of the charter pilots and could take the crates on the next flight that afternoon to Los Rodeos, if the paperwork was ready, but the fisherman said that the crates of squid had to go somewhere else first. Rafa was obviously pleased to have an audience and was happy to explain where and how they caught the squid. He did, however, seem rather fed up and Chano discovered that was because he had to work late that night. Chano listened sympathetically and asked why they had to go fishing at night. Was that because squid were nocturnal and you could only catch them at night?

Suddenly Rafa looked worried and clammed up unexpectedly. Chano was slightly taken aback but had enough sense not to pursue the matter. Instead he just grinned and offered to help him load the seven crates of squid into the old truck. Rafa accepted gratefully and they chatted some more about squid and octopus fishing. They parted on good terms and Rafa waved as he drove away.

Some time later Felix came along the quay to his boat. Seeing Chano, he smiled and wished him good day. Chano realised quickly that this must be Pedro's brother because of the similarity in features, but this fisherman seemed a much more friendly chap.

'Hello! Are you going squid fishing today?'

'No. No. The squid seem to have disappeared, so I don't bother with them any more,' replied Felix sociably. 'My son and I do sightseeing trips for the tourists now.'

'Really! I was just talking to the fisherman off that new boat over there and he was packing up seven crates of squid in ice. I offered to fly them to Tenerife this afternoon, as I usually do, but he said the squid had to go somewhere else first.'

'What! You were talking to my brother, Pedro?' asked Felix in surprise.

'No. No, Rafa, the chap who works for him, I presume. He said they fish off the western coast near a place called La Dama and they feed the squid regularly to make sure they have a good easy supply whenever they need them.'

'Well, I'll be damned,' said Felix. 'The crafty old devil! No wonder I can't catch any of the wretched squid!'

'They are going out tonight as well for some reason. I don't think they're fishing for squid though. Rafa wasn't too happy about it.'

'I don't suppose he was! By the way, how do you know my brother?'

'I see him at the airport. He meets the charter plane which Domingo and I fly and collects the conference delegates in the minibus. He looks like you, but you two are very different, aren't you?'

'I would hope so!' replied Felix with a grin. 'Have you time for a beer? I could drop you back to the airport afterwards, if you like.'

'I'd love to, but I haven't time today unfortunately. When I do, it will have to be a coffee, I'm afraid. As the pilot, I am not allowed to drink, even if I'm off duty for a few hours between flights and I can't afford to lose my licence. Another time perhaps! I just came into town as I had some free time, but I need to go back soon. Why don't you give me your mobile number and next time I can make it into town I'll give you a bell. If you're free as well, it would be great to spend some time together. You can tell me all about sport and commercial fishing. I know absolutely nothing about fishing but I'm a good listener. I'm Chano, by the way.'

'Good idea, Chano! I'm Felix. I'll just put your number into my mobile. I'll have to text you mine. I can never remember it. The youngsters seem to be able to rattle off ten or eleven digit numbers without any trouble but I can't. Too old for these modern inventions, I suppose.

It took me ages to learn how to text. My daughter was very patient teaching me how to use a mobile phone. I think she found it very amusing that I hadn't a clue what to do, but she had the good grace not to say so.'

'I think we all have trouble with these modern gadgets. Just when you have managed to operate one, an updated version comes on the market, which is even more complicated and sophisticated and you have to start the learning process all over again. Thank you so much for taking the time to chat to me. I do appreciate it. I've really enjoyed your company, Felix. It's been quite an education this morning at the harbour, I can tell you! I'll look forward to catching up with you again soon.'

'Please can you turn off left here and park, Satya? There's a lovely little cove down there a few hundred metres from a deserted village. The fish processing factory closed many years ago and there was no work here, so everyone left. Dad used to take us in his boat to the little cove when we were kids. It was our secret place, because it was only really accessible from the sea. Would you like to walk part way down to the village? The track is probably very rough now but there should be some spectacular views.'

Twenty minutes later they were sitting on a rocky outcrop overlooking the village. It was certainly a beautiful day and the clear blue sea shimmered in the afternoon heat.

'It was definitely worth stopping here, Ana. It's so picturesque. That ravine is so steep-sided and drops so dramatically down to the sea! What's the name of the village?'

'It's called La Rajita. We used to have picnics on the beach over there and then clamber back over the rocks. We spent some very happy hours here. It was always so very peaceful. This track down to the village is terrible now. You'd ruin the suspension if you drove down there, so I shouldn't think anyone much comes here now.'

They sat there quietly in the glorious sunshine, lazily watching the gentle swell. Lunch had been great fun and they had promised to do it again some time soon. Several pairs of laurel pigeons cooed to each other in the trees nearby.

'I don't think those pigeons over there are on the endangered list,' laughed Ana. 'Shame we didn't see a giant lizard. I was rather looking forward to that. They obviously weren't in the mood for sunbathing today on the ledges that we were able to observe. It's incredible they aren't extinct. I hope they manage to survive for centuries to come. In fact, thinking about it, there doesn't seem to be much wildlife around here at all.'

'There's some 'wildlife' moving down there,' said Satya suddenly, staring intently at the semi-derelict factory. 'Let's go a bit further down and see what's going on.'

They carefully negotiated the stony track until they had a better view of the deserted village and the shore.

'Good heavens! That's Uncle Pedro's old truck. That looks like Rafa, our friend who works for him. Whatever is he doing in La Rajita?'

'There are two other people down there. They are unloading crates from the truck and taking them into the factory. It all looks a bit shady to me!'

'Could well be! Uncle Pedro has several shady fingers in many fishy pies. Let's not think about him and spoil this lovely day! Let's go back to the car and I'll show you some more of this lovely island.'

Ana laughed and they set off hand in hand up the steep track back to the car. Satya was great company. This was the best weekend she had ever had. How wonderful that her Mum had procured that job for her at the Centre. She would enjoy every minute of it. She guessed that the Professor would dispense with her services quite summarily, if he could recruit an Indian secretary. He evidently had a very low opinion of the Islanders. She knew her work was accurate, because she checked it thoroughly, but the Professor never praised her, never criticised her. In fact, he rarely spoke to her at all. It felt sometimes as if she did not exist as a human being, just a robot regurgitating documents.

Thank goodness Satya was there; he was such a warm and caring person. She was very lucky. Working at the Centre was a phenomenal experience in more ways than one.

⁂

After Chano had delivered his passengers and luggage safely to the terminal at Los Rodeos he taxied over to the hangar, where he was to rendezvous with Domingo. They wanted to discuss holiday plans. His fellow pilot was there already and they chatted amicably as they walked back to the terminal building for a coffee. Chano told him about his experiences that morning down by the harbour, about the squid fishing and meeting Felix, who was so much more gentle and friendly than his brother, Pedro. Then Chano commented that it was strange that he always collected the empty crates in Los Rodeos and took them back to La Gomera, whereas Domingo always transported the full crates of squid to Tenerife.

'You're right. I've never really thought about that before. It's almost as though we're not supposed to meet up. Where do you think that the crates of squid go from the airport? I just assumed they went to some posh hotel in the capital and ended up on the menu. Did you know you could fry squid, you can eat it raw as sashimi and you can have it marinated or even braise the horrible stuff? It's full of protein and iron and very healthy, as long as you don't eat the tentacles, as they are high in cholesterol.'

Chano stared at his friend in amazement and grinned mischievously.

'You are a veritable mine of useless information, Domingo! I've never given it a thought either. I just obey the instructions we're given. As long as all the paperwork is in order, I don't care what we transport. I do remember that I once volunteered to drop off a couple of crates at a clinic near the airport because the courier was ill and there was a great panic on. It was on my way home anyway, so I didn't particularly mind. I was rather surprised at the time that the squid wasn't going to a hotel, but a clinic would make sense. If squid is so good for you, then it would help patients convalescing in the clinic after operations, wouldn't it?'

'I suppose so. I think that eating squid after an operation would make me feel much worse! I'd rather have ice-cream and lots of it!'

'So would I! Where was the squid from the harbour going today?'

'I don't know. The fisherman packing it into the crates was very guarded and obviously didn't want to say too much, so I didn't press him. He seemed quite uneasy about it all, though.'

'There is definitely something fishy going on! This squid is becoming quite intriguing! Perhaps we ought to do a 'squid hunt' on our holiday. We could go to that weird forest at Garajonay that you were telling me about and then head towards the coast for some exploring near La Dama where all these squid are caught. We never see much of the western coast from the air, so it would be totally new to us. What do you think?'

'Why not? You never know what mystery we might unravel! *CHANO-DOMINGO & CO, Squid-Hunting Detectives!* I bet no other detective has been on a squid investigation! It would be an interesting theme for our walking holiday, don't you think? It could be a lot of fun.'

'On one condition! I don't want to eat any of the hideous stuff, if you don't mind. Once in a lifetime tackling squid on a dinner plate is more than enough! I fancy some nice local soup with home-made bread just out of the oven and lots of fresh fruit. Perhaps a few days of a healthier lifestyle will break a few of the bad habits I've got into. Sitting in a cockpit all day long and then take-away meals at the end of the shift is not good for my metabolism. I need more fresh air and exercise.'

'So do I!' agreed his friend. 'I'm very unfit, too. I'm really looking forward to our hiking holiday, squid or no squid.'

Satya dropped Ana off at her house and thanked her warmly for a wonderful day. On cloud nine, Ana sailed into the sitting-room, where her mother was engrossed in some French translation work.

'Hi Mum! I've had the most amazing day! Have you had a good time too?'

Maria smiled at her radiant daughter and replied that she and Dad had had a relaxing time together and had still managed to do quite a lot.

'You really enjoy translation work, don't you Mum?'

'Yes, I do, darling. It feels as though my brain has come alive again and it's nice to be appreciated for one's intelligence rather than for one's activities with a floor polisher.'

'You are always appreciated, Mum, even if we forget to show it sometimes. Where's Dad? What's he been up to?'

'He just popped down the street to see Juan and Sara. Juan wanted to know how the new venture was coming on.'

'That's kind of him. I'm glad it's working out so well for Dad and Sandro. I know it's early days, but the future looks a lot brighter for Dad now, doesn't it Mum?'

'Yes, it does, thank goodness. Dad was becoming very depressed about the squid fishing and just didn't know what to try next. It's ironic that a suggestion from Sandro should revolutionise the business. He who hated fish and boats and all who sailed in them! If Uncle Pedro hadn't annoyed him so much, he would either still be a lifeguard or working for Uncle Pedro and we'd still be worrying about him.'

'That must be the only good thing Uncle Pedro has ever done for us,' said Ana smiling at her mother.

'You're right. By the way, Dad has cracked your email code for you, but I think he'd like to go through the messages with you himself, as there are still bits and pieces to puzzle out. He's working tomorrow morning but back here for lunch. Perhaps you two could sit down together then?'

'Great! I'll just check my emails before I go to bed. Perhaps there's a reply from Tamarai, that Indian girl whose father is missing. I simply can't imagine what she's going through. I wonder why the Professor never bothered to reply to her emails?'

'Hey! Sandro! Guess what I found out this morning when I was down at the harbour! Our beloved Uncle Pedro has been deliberately feeding the squid off the rocks at La Dama. That's why I couldn't catch any. The disloyal creatures deserted my fishing grounds in favour of a free meal from Pedro.'

'How did you find that out, Dad?'

'Quite by chance, actually. A very pleasant fellow called Chano had been talking to Rafa. He saw him packing the squid in ice into crates and started chatting to him about fishing techniques. I expect poor Rafa was delighted to have someone to talk to. Pedro can't be much company. Fancy feeding the squid with mackerel to make them stay in that location! Uncle Pedro's a crafty old devil, isn't he?'

'He certainly is, Dad. That would also explain why we see so many dolphins on our charter trips up the west coast, wouldn't it? The dolphins would be attracted to that area to eat the squid, which are eating the mackerel. Oh, well, that's one mystery solved. It's good business for us. Word has gone round the hotels and the bars that if you want to see any dolphins, our boat is the best option. The west coast trips are much more popular than the east coast ones. Shall we drop those from our advertising leaflet?'

'Yes, I should think so. We seem to be doing quite well with the sport fishing too. The moray eels are being very obliging and taking the bait we offer them.'

'Those Germans came out with us three times in one week and finally managed to land a moray eel. They were thrilled. I expect the photographs they took are all over the internet now. Free advertising for us! It's great!'

'I must take Rafa for a few beers and thank him for letting us use the rods. I didn't really want to incur any expenses on new projects until all the old business debts had been cleared. Those rods and reels would have been fairly costly if we'd had to buy them. I know you offered to buy them with your savings, Sandro, which was very kind and generous of you, but we need to be cautious. The sport fishing idea might have been a non-starter and we could have lost even more money.

Next month we can review the situation and see what it is best to invest our time, money and energy into. Are you sure you are still happy doing this, Sandro? Don't you miss your work as a lifeguard?'

'Not at all, Dad. I was very, very bored on the beach all day with stupid holidaymakers who ignored all the safety signs. It was a very superficial sort of job. There was no future in it. I know all the family were telling me that right from the beginning, but I was too stubborn and stupid and wouldn't listen. I thought I had the perfect job and didn't want to admit that I was wrong. At least now I'm using my brain. I love doing the commentary in English for the sightseeing trips. I'm so glad Mum insisted that we talk English at home all the time. I used to think it was a real pain in the neck and totally unnecessary but it's turned out to be a fantastic asset and it's great to be able to use it to our advantage. Well done, Mum! Now I can see a proper future. This could be a really successful business venture. Above all, I can see a fantastic working partnership. We get on really well now, don't we Dad?'

'Not bad at all! I can't believe we're actually working together on the boat. Mum and Ana still can't believe it either. Secretly, I think they are delighted, but they don't want to stop teasing us for quite a while yet. They're having far too much fun!'

Down at the harbour Pedro and Rafa were preparing for their evening expedition. Anger and thwarted ambition lined Pedro's miserable weather-beaten face. Bitter resentment lurked in his evil, dark eyes revealing a cold-blooded callousness, which inspired fear and distrust in most people who had the misfortune to come into contact with him. He grunted orders at Rafa, who obeyed in silence. There was no point in antagonising his despicable employer when he was in such a foul mood. Hopefully, tonight's trip would be calm and easy and he would be back in time for his favourite television programme. He knew that he could quite easily disappear at sea without trace, if he ever queried orders from Pedro. A watery death was no idle threat, so Rafa wisely asked no questions and kept his opinions to himself. Blackmail was also rather a powerful deterrent. His wife's medical care had been very expensive. Pedro had caught him off guard and was now exploiting the situation to the full. Rafa was paying dearly for his mistake. He didn't know exactly what was going on, but he didn't like any of these late night 'rescues' and would have preferred the good old days of ordinary fishing trips in his own fishing boat, which he had been forced to sell to settle debts. He wished he could go and work for someone else, but he had a nasty feeling that Pedro wouldn't take at all kindly to that idea.

'Sandro, does your friend, Antonio, still work at the main hospital in Tenerife? I am trying to help this Indian girl, Tamarai, to trace her father. She says he is a surgeon and was on an eighteen-month contract in Tenerife. He should have gone back to India some time ago, but they haven't heard from him. Apparently he was working on some top-secret research, so communication was fairly limited anyway. He was saving all his salary so that he could set up a clinic back in Chennai to help the poor workers in the area, whilst doing special surgery on the rich to fund it. He seems to be a sort of 21stcentury Robin Hood.'

'He sounds a nice guy, Ana. I don't think Antonio works at the hospital any more. I think he has a better paid job at that posh new Clinic near the airport, but I'm sure he still has lots of contacts at the hospital. I'll text him now, if you like, and ask him to try to trace this Indian doctor.'

'Great! Thank you! His name is Karthik Nayar. He is 53 years old and has very long fingers! That's probably why he is such a good surgeon! Apparently, he always attracts comments and various nicknames from the nurses and other doctors because of his hands, so perhaps someone will remember him more easily. He was always well-liked and popular. His family is terrified that something awful has happened to him.'

'Okay, Ana! Text is winging its way to Antonio, as we speak. I'll let you know as soon as I hear anything from him.'

Domingo staggered up the rocky outcrop at the top of Mount Garajonay, the highest point on the island, and joined Chano, who was trying to get his breath back.

'Would you believe we could be so unfit? Too much sitting around in cosy cockpits and not enough exercise! We're puffing like decrepit old steam trains. At least it should be easier going down.'

'I wouldn't count on that! It's often worse going downhill. It will probably kill our knees and calf muscles and we'll ache in all sorts of strange places tomorrow!'

'I'm already aching in strange places,' said Domingo groaning, as he sat down to recover from his exertions.

'Wow, what an amazing view! Look at those strange distorted laurel trees and weird rock formations! All those deep forested valleys we've seen from the air and the steep rocky coastline. It's fascinating to see it all at close quarters. It was almost worth the agony of staggering up here!'

'Come on! What are a few aches and pains compared to that superb view?'

They decided to rest for a while near the summit and celebrate their achievement with a rather lukewarm beer and some fresh bread and local cheese, before they tackled the way-marked route along to the western edge of the forest and on down to the coast.

'Well done, Martin. You're a quick learner. You can whistle better than I can. Just concentrate on these two phrases: 'Help' and 'Come quickly!' Practise until you're perfect! You never know when you might need them! And don't use them on the girls or you'll have my Uncle Pedro to deal with.'

'Scary! I definitely don't want to upset your Uncle Pedro. He positively exudes evil and fills me with a tremendous urge to keep as far away from him as possible. So, I'll just practise whistling in the bath for the time being.'

'Good! I'm relieved to hear it. Fancy a beer? My throat is amazingly dry after all that whistling. Let's try that new bar down by the harbour!'

'I'm so glad you suggested this holiday, Domingo. I'm really enjoying it, even if I do complain a bit. Fresh air, freedom, sleeping under the stars! Great company! What more could we ask for?'

'Muscles that weren't sore, for a start! That was quite a steep slog down the slopes of that ravine to the beach here. My knees haven't stopped shaking yet and I've got muscular pain in places I didn't even know I had muscles! No, you're right. I'm very glad we're here. I think we needed a break. We've had a very hectic fortnight hopping round the Islands, taking the Professor and the conference delegates around here there and everywhere. Not to mention that thoroughly obnoxious, arrogant businessman, our other frequent flier, who acts as though he owns the charter plane and all who fly in it. Personally, I reckon he has a lover somewhere on Lanzarote, because he seems to go there so regularly. He also spends a lot of time on Gran Canaria as well. I don't know what connection he has with the Conference Centre, if any. He never talks about any of the projects. He gives me the creeps but at least he keeps us in a job! Anyway, it's good to stop rushing around and just relax for a while. Here, have another drink!'

It was very peaceful in the mouth of the little cave. When they had finally reached the beach, they had seen the old fish factory and tiny village. They decided not to camp near it. They both wanted to be further away from any signs of civilization, even though it did all appear to be deserted. They had, therefore, scrambled over large basalt boulders to reach the cave where they were now happily ensconced. Darkness had long since closed in around them, but they were perfectly happy reminiscing about their exploits flying round the Canary Islands.

'You know, Domingo, I have a gut feeling that there's something funny going on in these Islands. I was checking the passenger lists and freight manifests for last month when I was filling in my time-sheets and there were quite a few discrepancies between the number of delegates arriving in Tenerife for onward transfer to that posh new Conference Centre and the number departing, especially our Asian friends. I even checked with my friend, Alfredo, at Tenerife Passport Control at the main airport and he confirmed that there were unexplained discrepancies. I know it's really none of our business but some of the Indians do seem to vanish into thin air, whereas I could account for all the European and American delegates. Even when we take all the Americans and Eastern Europeans to Lanzarote, they all fly back with us next day. For some strange reason the Indians never go to Lanzarote. Perhaps the Indians go back by boat for some reason. But why would they, when there is a charter plane service especially for them?'

'Yes, that is a little odd. Can't say I've really noticed. Perhaps the Indians eat too much squid and have to convalesce for a while!'

'Perhaps. That's an interesting theory! But why just the Indian passengers? They have the same food at the hotel as the other delegates, so why should they become ill?'

'Don't know. One strange thing struck me the other day as well. The Conference Centre is supposed to be sponsoring loads of environmental and alternative energy projects around the Islands including research into wind power and solar power and any other sort of power they can dream up but I can't say that I've seen much evidence of these projects from the air. Have you noticed anything?'

'No, nothing at all. You're right. That is peculiar, isn't it? The delegates are always talking about climate change and alternative sources of energy and conservation when they're on the plane. Any installations ought to be visible from the air, yet neither of us has spotted anything. Let's face it! There's enough solar power here for half of Africa and there's plenty of wind power for the other half! As for wave energy, just look at the huge breakers over there thumping those enormous rocks!'

'Wow! Just look at the spray! The wind has obviously strengthened quite a bit while we've been talking, but we're quite sheltered here in this cave so we haven't noticed it. I'm glad we're not flying tonight. I was delayed for three hours the other day because of strong winds and didn't make it home until midnight.'

'Hey! Did you see that? Someone just flashed a light in front of that old building near the shore. I'm sure of it! I thought the village was deserted and we had the place to ourselves. That looked like a signal of some sort. I wonder what's going on. This is getting exciting! Come on, Detective, let's go squid-hunting!'

Martin and Sandro were on their second beer. Martin was regaling his friend with details of his exploits at a wild beach party the night before, but Sandro wasn't paying any attention. He was almost mesmerized by the lights of a fishing boat coming back into the harbour nearby. That was Uncle Pedro's boat; he was sure of it. Why on earth would he be out so late at night? Something illegal, no doubt. Thank goodness, he had not gone to work for Uncle Pedro. He must have been mad to have even considered it.

'Hello! Planet Earth to Sandro! You haven't heard a word I've said, have you Sandro?'

'No. Sorry mate. I was just trying to work something out. What were you saying?'

Half an hour later Sandro returned home. He wasn't in the right mood for party talk, so he had left Martin to chat up the two German girls who had come into the bar. There were more important issues to consider now than girls and beer. Not that he had thought that three months ago! He grunted a greeting to his mother in the kitchen and then went into the sitting-room, where he flopped in the armchair near the computer desk where Ana was checking her emails. He greeted her somewhat absent-mindedly. He was just making himself comfortable when his mobile vibrated impatiently in the pocket of his jeans. He fished it out half-heartedly, ready to delete the text message. Instead he sat bolt upright, read through the long text and said to his sister:

'Ana, I've just had some info back from Antonio.'

'Fantastic, Sandro. Has he managed to find out anything about the surgeon?'

'Yes, in a roundabout way. Your surgeon never actually worked at the main hospital in Tenerife. Turns out he was actually working at that new Clinic where Antonio now works. Some highly paid hush-hush project, by all accounts. Antonio says he was a friendly chap and he worked very long hours. Then there was a big bust-up and he left.'

'What was the bust-up about? Did Antonio say?'

'He says it was something about incompatibility but no-one talks about it and the staff all clammed up when he tried to find out more details. He says there was obviously a clash of personalities for some reason and the surgeon felt he couldn't work at the Clinic any longer. Perhaps he was tired or homesick as well and didn't need the stress any more.'

'Do they know where he went?'

'Everyone assumed he went back to India. He just disappeared that evening with all his belongings in a car with a driver and another passenger. That was just over three weeks ago. That's all Antonio was able to find out. It's not a lot of help, Ana.'

'It's more than we knew before. Please thank him for me, Sandro. I'll email Tamarai and update her with what we know. She's going to be very upset but I'll promise her that we'll keep on trying to locate her father. At least some news is good news, I suppose. Her father was obviously alive and well three weeks ago. We'll have to see if we can trace which flight he took. I don't suppose the authorities will give us any information because of data protection laws. Perhaps Dad will know a way round that little problem.'

'Let's stay out of sight behind this rock! I don't think this has anything to do with squid, unfortunately! It looks like something seriously illegal is going on and I think we might be wise to keep a low profile, since we are rather inexperienced at this detective lark!'

'I can just make out a boat over there by the rocks. I hope it's not in trouble. It's difficult to see very much in the darkness with all this spray flying about.'

'Look there's the torchlight signal again. There seems to be an old wooden jetty of sorts over there by those huge rocks and the boat is trying to come alongside it.'

'Keep well down! Someone is flashing a signal again from that derelict building and the skipper of the boat has signalled back. It's obviously all pre-arranged. There's evidently smuggling going on here and the situation might become very violent if they discover they have an audience. We don't want to be in the line of fire. This detective business is turning out to be quite scary. I can't cope with this adrenaline rush. I think I'd rather stick to flying.'

'Yes, me too, though it's a bit late to say that now!' Domingo whispered back.

They crouched down in their improvised hiding-place and waited in the sombre night, hardly daring to breathe. It seemed ages before something happened but when it did, it was the last thing either of them had expected.

The makeshift ambulance drew up at the rear entrance of the Conference Hotel and two men emerged. They said not a word to Juan as they rushed past him. Eventually two people were bundled unceremoniously into the back of the vehicle with their luggage and whisked off into the darkness. The porter watched the van disappear and shook his head in disbelief. Surely these rich Indians deserved better treatment than that. He didn't like them; if truth be told, he didn't like any foreigners very much, even though the Islanders' livelihood depended on the tourists. The new Indian Conference Centre had however provided his family with stable employment and he was grateful for that, so he had no intention of voicing his opinions to anyone except his wife. He just couldn't believe what had happened to two of the hotel's guests. Any guest who was ill should have had better care than that. They paid for the best and they should have the best. He could imagine what his wife Sara would say when he relayed the sorry tale to her.

※

Ana had just finishing emailing Tamarai when a text announced itself on her mobile phone. Ana read it through and could barely contain her excitement as she relayed the message to her mother.

'Mum! Satya has invited me to go lizard-hunting with him again. Isn't that smashing?'

'They didn't call it lizard-hunting in my day!'

'We're just friends,' laughed Ana. 'We knew it was highly unlikely we would see one of the giant lizards, but we had a lot of fun looking! I've lived on this island all my life and yet I know so little about its flora and fauna. I think Satya is enjoying teaching me,' concluded Ana.

'I bet he is!' They were both howling with laughter when Felix arrived home and poked his head round the door.

※

Painful cramp was working its way down Domingo's thigh muscles and he longed to stretch out his long legs but Chano motioned to him not to move an inch, as the passengers who had disembarked from the boat tried to scramble over the rocks uncomfortably close to where they were hiding. Someone was shouting 'hotel' and the group headed purposefully, if extremely unsteadily, across the slippery black boulders and towards the building where the light was flashing. Not much of a hotel, thought Domingo, if they couldn't afford to turn the lights on to welcome their guests. Strange guests who arrived with no luggage in the dead of night!

It seemed an eternity until the danger had passed and they could emerge from their uncomfortable hiding-place. Domingo massaged his thigh and cramped calf muscles vigorously. Chano complained volubly about his stiff neck and aching upper torso which had been forced into such an unnaturally squashed position behind both Domingo and the rock where they had crouched for so long.

'Whew! That was a close call. We came here to hunt squid, not human beings. Whatever is going on? The occupants of that boat were Africans and a very poor bedraggled lot they were. They were so weak they could barely walk and they didn't have any personal possessions with them. They weren't going to a hotel, despite what that fisherman was yelling. There isn't one within ten miles of here.'

'No, there isn't. Did you see that those two men waiting for them on the beach were carrying what looked suspiciously like shot-guns? They didn't look very friendly even from this distance. The whole scene was decidedly scary. We must be looking at a case of modern slave-trading or sex-trafficking, I should think,' added his friend.

'I think I've had enough of playing detective for one night. I think we ought to make our way out of here if we can, as unobtrusively as possible. It might be a den of iniquity or worse in that building. We certainly couldn't relax if we stayed here now after what we've witnessed. If we ever did manage to get off to sleep, we'd have terrible nightmares for a start and be scared stiff into the bargain.'

'I couldn't agree with you more. Let's collect our stuff from the cave and scarper. Once we have a safe distance between us and the trigger-happy 'hotel' staff on the beach over there we can work out what to do. In any case, we can't contact the authorities here because we won't have any mobile signal under the cliffs. Oh heck! We'll have to puff and pant up that wretched ravine again. Just what my muscles want at this time of night! The skipper could obviously contact the people on the beach by mobile, but we have several deep valleys between us and any help.'

'Okay partner! Let's proceed with the utmost caution. At least there's no moonlight so our shadows will be less noticeable. There is far too much excitement down here tonight and I'll be very glad to get as far away as possible. Look on the bright side! Think how fit we'll be when we get back.'

'Okay partner! Let's get out of here pronto! Onwards and upwards!'

Next morning Ana and Felix were relaxing in wooden deckchairs enjoying the late morning sunshine in their small courtyard. Maria had very kindly just brought them coffee but didn't join them as she knew they would be engrossed in deciphering the emails together and would not want to waste time chattering about inessentials. Moreover, she had promised to visit Sara and cheer her up, as she had been unwell the last few days. She gazed fondly for a few minutes at her daughter and husband working quietly together, before returning to the kitchen, wrapping up a freshly decorated sponge cake for Sara and picking up some recent photos of the family to amuse her. She closed the cottage door quietly behind her and set off for her friend's house.

'Oh! Maria! Thank you so much for popping round! It's so good to see you. I do love our natters. Juan was working late shift last night. He was exhausted when he came home and quite upset—I'll tell you about that in a minute—so I told him to have a lie-in and I'd wake him up in time for a late lunch. Then he can relax watching the football this afternoon before he has to go back to work tonight. So, as you can see, I'm sort of home alone. The boys are on a hiking trip with their mates and probably won't be back till late so I am absolutely delighted to have your company. You couldn't have timed it better.

'It's lovely to see you, Sara. Are you on the mend?'

'I feel quite bright in the mornings, but I'm still easily tired and haven't much energy.'

'Let me make you a nice cup of coffee and I brought some cake to go with it. I thought it might tempt your appetite.'

'It certainly would. Thank you, Maria. You are always so kind and thoughtful. You're a real tonic!'

'Wow, Dad! You did incredibly well to decipher this lot. Thank you so much. I would never have managed it on my own and I would have worried about it all.'

'Can't have you worrying, young lady. I quite enjoyed doing it. It's good to use your intellectual faculties after doing purely physical work all day. I don't use my brain enough. I ought to do much more. Your Mother always has her nose in a book and seems to get a lot of pleasure out of reading everything she can lay her hands on.'

'I love reading, too, Dad. It never ceases to amaze me how much you can learn from a well-written book. Anyway, back to these emails. Like you said, I don't think any of them are relevant to the environmental projects that the Centre is involved with or any of the conferences coming up. It all seems to be about recent medical developments and special storage techniques. It doesn't specify what they want to store or why. There are a lot of technical terms like 'nephropathy', 'immuno-suppressive therapy' and 'keratoplasty' which I don't understand and have never seen before but I can look the medical terms up and make sure that all this has nothing to do with my work for the Professor. I don't want him dressing me down in public for having omitted to do something properly. He can be very cruel, almost callous sometimes and I don't want to end up as his next victim and burst into tears in front of him. That would be so humiliating. I want to stay cool, calm and collected at all times and I'll just sob my heart out in private! It's much better for my image as efficient secretary!'

'I'm sure you are very efficient from what your mother tells me! Actually, I don't understand why these messages were encrypted in the first place. It looks just like ordinary technical medical data. It's not as though this information would be useful for terrorists or criminals.'

'Perhaps it's new research and hasn't been published yet and they want to protect their copyright or patent it or whatever they do,' suggested Ana.

'I don't know,' replied her father. 'There's also this very cryptic note at the end of one of the emails which I haven't fathomed out yet and I don't like to be defeated by a puzzle!'

'Gosh! It looks rather mathematical, doesn't it? Definitely not my strong subject. Shall we ask Sandro to have a look at it, now that he has finally decided to wake up his brain cells? I think Maths was one of the few subjects he actually enjoyed and worked hard at.'

'Good idea,' replied her father, smiling and frowning almost simultaneously as he remembered vividly the constant battles they'd had with Sandro and education.

'You were going to tell me why Juan was upset last night.'

'Oh yes, so I was! I keep forgetting things nowadays. Well, I don't actually forget them. I just don't remember them when I should.'

'Don't worry about it, Sara. We all do it! I hate to think what we'll be like when we are in our seventies!'

'Me, too, Maria. At least that's still twenty years or more away for both of us. Perhaps the scientists will have developed a technique by then for implanting new memory cells or regenerating the old ones. I think we're going to need them. By the way, that sponge cake was stunning. I don't know how you make them so light. Mine always sulk not long after I put them into the oven. Instead of rising as light as a feather like yours, they flop into the cake tin like deflated balloons and I have to turn them into trifles and soak them in brandy.

Then I pretend that was what I had intended to make in the first instance. The family all know they were failed sponge cakes but they are very diplomatic. They think it's wiser to say nothing and just enjoy the brandy fruit trifles!'

'I must remember that strategy, Sara. I don't think my family is as well trained as yours. I think my son would tease me mercilessly for days or even weeks!'

―※―

Satya was at his desk in the small suite he had been allocated in the Conference Centre Hotel. It was modern but it certainly wasn't very homely. In fact, it was quite anonymous, but at least it came with the job. This position as Executive Co-ordinator of Research was not exactly what he had envisaged, but at least he was being well paid and could live in the Hotel permanently on half-board for free, so he was able to save almost all of his salary. His contract had another five months to run and then he would be off to pastures new to involve himself in another worthwhile project, with hopefully a more amenable Director of Studies. The only problem was, he mused, he didn't really want pastures new, not now that that marvellous girl, Ana, had come on the scene. She positively sparkled with wit and enthusiasm and made the days pass so quickly and enjoyably. She teased him mercilessly and he loved every minute of it. In fact, he loved her. Where had that thought just come from? He had promised himself he wasn't going to fall in love until he had published some acclaimed academic papers. Unfortunately, the heart rarely obeyed the head. He pushed delightful thoughts of Ana aside and duly bent his head to the research reports from Jeevan and Amit, which he was collating. He reflected that data on rare mosses, lichens and lizards was hardly likely to shake the academic world. Still, he'd better get it finished before he picked Ana up for lunch.

'Do you remember me telling you last week about the six Indian guests who arrived unexpectedly at the Hotel?' Sara confided in Maria. 'Well, we all had to rush round like mad things and make the beds and double clean the rooms. Why we had to do that I don't know; we clean them all well the first time round; it's insulting to be made to do it again. That's probably what made me ill. I was really tired anyway and just coming off shift when your grumpy brother-in-law rolled up in that posh new minibus of his with six Indian gentlemen. No-one knew they were coming and it was panic stations. The receptionist had the day off so Juan stepped in and asked the Indian guests to sit in the lounge and relax until the rooms were ready. The last of the delegates had left two days before and there were eight days free before the next lot arrived, so we were taking the opportunity to spring-clean the rooms, a floor at a time. Consequently, nothing was ready when the Indian gentlemen turned up. The chef wasn't very pleased either, as he had just cleared out all the fridges and freezers, so he had to send out for fresh food for the guests. Not that they ate much, anyway. Waste of time cooking for them. Nothing seemed to tempt their appetite and they wasted so much food. Chef was very cross. The staff enjoyed it though and cheered him up by eating every delicacy in sight and telling him how delicious it all was.'

Sara paused in her narrative and glanced anxiously at the clock. Plenty of time yet before she had to prepare a late lunch. Maria smiled at her friend and urged her to continue.

'Um, where was I? Oh yes! Well, two of the Indian guests looked like death warmed up and seemed to get worse as the week went on, despite all the wonderful food Chef was producing for them. Juan wanted to ring for a doctor because he was so worried about them but he has strict instructions to always inform the Centre manager before he does anything. So he rang him and after a lot of to-ing and fro-ing the manager called him back some time later and told him he had arranged for an ambulance. Queer sort of ambulance, it was! Anyway, this old van turned up at the rear entrance of the hotel late that night. Two men rushed out and took charge of the two Indian guests. Juan couldn't believe his eyes when the men just bundled the two Indians and their belongings into the back of the van and drove off without a civil word. He was totally speechless and extremely upset. I mean, we pride ourselves on the hospitality we offer to our guests.'

'Why use the rear entrance of the hotel? That seems very odd.'
'Yes, that's what Juan thought. I mean those delegates pay top whack to stay in that hotel and if they're ill, you'd think a proper ambulance would come and take them to the hospital in San Sebastian. Juan doesn't think they went there, 'cos they turned left at the end of the road, not right. Juan was proper upset by it all, I can tell you.'
'I hope they get better soon wherever they've gone. It can't be very pleasant being ill so far from home. Perhaps they'll come back to the hotel when they've recovered.'
'Perhaps! Watch this space! Anyway, I'd better start getting lunch ready and then wake up Juan. Thank you so much, Maria, for coming. You have cheered me up no end and your cake was gorgeous.'
'I hope it won't spoil your lunch. Say 'hello' to Juan and the boys for me. Take care and don't overdo it, Sara.

Meanwhile back at their homely cottage, Ana was getting ready to go out to lunch with Satya. She suddenly thought of the missing surgeon and her promise to Tamarai.

'Dad, how could we find out if this Indian surgeon caught a flight out of Tenerife? I know we can't find out officially, but do you have any contacts at the airports who might be persuaded to help us?'

'No. Sorry, Ana. Not any more. Can't help you there, I'm afraid. Hey! Hang on a moment! I might be able to find out some info for you. That friendly chap, Chano, I was chatting to at the harbour last week said he was a pilot. He might know someone who could help. What was the surgeon's name?'

'Karthik Nayar. I'll write it down for you. You could even practise texting, Dad, if you haven't already forgotten all I taught you! Thanks, Dad. I must go. Satya's waiting.

⧽

Chano and Domingo gathered up their rucksacks and stepped down off the bus.

'I think a large black coffee is called for after all that non-productive hassle, don't you?'

'Definitely and something warm and very filling to eat as well. I'm absolutely starving after all that exercise. At least we've walked off some of our frustration. I can't believe the police weren't in the slightest bit interested in our story. I thought they'd be rushing over to that old factory with half of the policemen on the

Island. Apparently they don't care whether it's people smuggling, slave trading or sex-trafficking. Why not? Because it involves Africans and they are seemingly not important. They come; they go; no-one cares! Africans do, however, have human rights, same as the rest of us.'

'Calm down, Domingo, or you'll undo all the relaxation of the holiday. Not that the last night was very relaxing. That was plain scary and very strenuous!'

'You would have thought that the police would at least have been interested in the guns, wouldn't you?'

'They probably thought we were making it all up. Africans, flashing signals, fishing boat, armed guards, old factory in the middle of nowhere. I expect they thought we'd been drinking. In the cold light of day it all sounds highly implausible, doesn't it?'

'Yes, it does. But we both saw it all. We didn't imagine it and we're both fully compos mentis, I think!'

'Well, we've done our duty. I don't know who else we can inform. We'd probably have the same reaction from Immigration and Customs. They'll all think we're bonkers. I suppose we look a bit rough and unshaven.'

'People shouldn't judge by appearances. The police should have listened to us properly and not treated us like raving lunatics. I felt quite humiliated.'

'Well, let's forget about it all for the time being and find a decent restaurant, before my stomach thinks that my throat has been cut!'

Satya was listening attentively as Ana told him about her family. They were waiting for the main course (not squid, thank goodness.) He had somehow managed to escape squid and octopus and would be grateful if he could continue to do so. Ana had ordered *paella* for them both with *bienmesabe* to follow. This was apparently her favourite dessert made with almonds, lemon rind and eggs and she wanted him to try it. He didn't mind what he ate, so long as Ana was with him. The views of the bay from the restaurant were breathtaking and he was very relaxed and happy.

'Dad and Uncle Pedro grew up on the family farm. They are very different personalities and it was fairly obvious even before Grandfather died that they were never going to be able to work together on the farm. Pedro insisted on working on the farm and refused to consider anything else so Dad decided to work extra hard at his exams and try something else. He passed them with flying colours and went off to Barcelona University to read English. He couldn't afford to come home very often, as he had to work during the vacations to pay for his studies. His plan was to come back to the farm and start some business with English and tourism. That way Uncle Pedro could keep farming but they could effectively keep out of each other's way.

Of course, nothing ever works out the way you plan. When Dad finished his degree and came back to La Gomera, he discovered that Uncle Pedro had illegally sold off most of the farmland to rich property developers and had pocketed all the money. Grandma saw not a penny of it and she died of a broken heart, not because of the money per se, but because Uncle Pedro had behaved so abominably by selling off the family inheritance for his own personal gain and it wasn't even legally his to sell. She couldn't understand how he had managed to sell the land right under her nose when the documents were in her name. She went to the police, filled in loads of forms and complained bitterly, but they did nothing. She tried to get one of the other local solicitors to investigate the deception, but Pedro bribed him and he told Grandma that the transactions were now legally finished and there was nothing to be done. So Grandma changed her will and left the farmhouse and the few remaining hectares to Dad but Uncle Pedro refused to move out of the house, when Grandma died and we can't afford all the legal fees and litigation to have him evicted. He breaks the law all the time, you know, but seems to be untouchable. So poor old Dad hasn't received any of his inheritance. He's very calm and philosophical about it. He just quietly moved out of the farmhouse and rented a small cottage down near the harbour with Mum and that's where we grew up.'

'I assume that your parents met at University in Barcelona?'

'Yes, Mum was reading Spanish and English and they met in the third semester. They were inseparable.

They were madly in love. It was very romantic. Then Mum's family were tragically killed in a terrible road accident just after she graduated so she had no ties back in England. She decided to make a new life in the Canary Islands with Dad. The rest, as they say, is history.'

'Why is your Uncle Pedro so difficult?'
'Who knows? He has a big chip on his shoulder, well, more like half a tree actually, that Dad went to University and he didn't and he seems very antagonistic towards Mum as well because of that. Uncle Pedro hated school and played truant all the time, which upset Grandma. Of course, he ended up semi-literate and resents it bitterly now. He has never had a kind word for me; he finds girls useless except for sex and housework, but he has a soft spot for my brother, Sandro and he was desperately trying to persuade him to join his fishing business. Mum threatened Sandro with excommunication from everyone and everything and excruciating torture at the very least if he became involved in any of Uncle Pedro's illicit dealings! Fortunately, my brother came to his senses just in time and realised what Uncle Pedro was really like. We've been trying to tell him for years, but he wouldn't see it. Mum and Dad are so relieved, I can't tell you. It's so happy at home now with Dad and Sandro working so well together and not arguing all the time about dead-end jobs and planning for an intelligent future. It's like a miracle. The fear and the tension have

disappeared and everyone is so much more relaxed, now that we know that Sandro is safe from Uncle Pedro's grasp and on the straight and narrow.'

Maria came into the kitchen to find her husband sitting at the table cursing under his breath. He was obviously trying to text on his mobile phone and it wasn't quite going to plan. He hadn't noticed her come in and carried on muttering for a while. She decided she had better put him out of his misery and offer her assistance.

'Damn modern gadgets! The keys are far too small for my big awkward fingers. I keep hitting the wrong key or else I press it too hard and end up with three of one letter and two of another when I don't want that. Then I press 'delete' instead of 'clear' to correct it all and the screen goes blank and I have to start all over again.'

'Let me do it for you, Felix. It'll be much quicker. Tell me what you want to say.'

'Thanks, Maria, but I'm doing something for Ana and since she spent hours teaching me how to text on this wretched mobile, I'd better do it or she won't be a happy bunny and will tease me for weeks. I ought to be able to use the perishing mobile, didn't I?'

'Okay, but I'm here if you need any help.'

Maria retreated smiling into the courtyard and buried herself in her translation work.

─≳─

Satya was tucking eagerly into the dessert when he suddenly thought of something.

'Ana, I meant to tell you! You remember I collected that report from the hut near Garajonay on our first outing? Well, I was re-reading it this morning and frankly, it wasn't very exciting or useful but Jeevan mentioned in passing that little village we saw from the road, La Rajita. Talking about your Uncle Pedro just now reminded me, because you thought you saw his old truck there. Jeevan said he had understood the village was deserted but he had noticed an old white van going up and down the track when he was camouflaged trying to spot the lizards and there was also some activity on the shore by that old fish factory. Jeevan seems to have been quite intrigued and decided to investigate further. I think the lizard-hunting must be quite boring and it was good to have a diversion. Anyway, he enlisted Amit's help and they have been keeping the site under surveillance for quite a while. They always parked well out of sight, found a good vantage point and waited patiently, keeping one eye on the cliffs for the lizards and one eye on the two people coming and going. They don't think anyone ever spotted them.'

'I love a mystery,' said Ana dreamily eating her favourite sweet.

'That dessert was delicious. Would you like coffee, Ana?'

'No thanks, Satya. What did Jeevan and Amit discover after all these hours of working as detectives? Did they even see a lizard?'

'No! Not a single one! We have actually started worrying about the lizards. We know they're rare and elusive but by the law of averages, you should get a few sightings when you have the area under surveillance for so long.'

'Satya, stop playing with me and tell me about the people and the old fish factory.'

'I was just answering your question about the lizards, Ana. Are you sure you wouldn't like a coffee?'

'You are being infuriating, Satya. I shall force-feed you squid and octopus in a moment, if you don't tell me! Don't keep me in suspense for one second longer!'

'Oh! No! Not squid! Not octopus! Okay, I give in! I'll put you out of your misery, young lady, though you may find the answer is rather less interesting than you thought.' 'Just tell me, Satya, for goodness sake! The suspense is killing me!'

'The truth is that they didn't really find out anything. The same two men went in and out in a battered old white vehicle every day at the same time. They left the factory down by the beach at noon, drove up to the main road, destination unknown, but probably heading towards Chipude and came back at half past two. They took it in turns to drive, so maybe they took it in turns to have a drink as well. Perhaps they went to lunch? No-one else went in or out of the factory, while they were watching. They have no idea what the two men were doing or why they should choose to do it there. Jeevan could hear a generator or some other machine humming when the men were in the building, but nothing else unusual happened at all. He doesn't know exactly what time the men arrived in the mornings or what time they left in the evenings. The vehicle was there before Amit arrived for his surveillance shifts and it was still there when Jeevan left after his. I'm afraid it's still rather a mystery.'

'Perhaps they're printing counterfeit currency or even making lizard pie!' Ana suggested mischievously. 'It's rather a miserable place to spend so much time. There are such lovely walks all round there and it's quite a good place to fish off the rocks. So why spend so much time in a derelict building? It doesn't make any sense. By the way, Satya, don't think for one moment that you have escaped torture by squid!'

Felix and Rafa were sitting outside one of the bars near the harbour. Rafa was sipping his beer gratefully and enjoying chatting about things in general.

'I wanted to thank you, Rafa, for letting us use those heavy duty sports rods and reels.'

'You're welcome to them. We weren't using them anyhow. They were just taking up space in the shed.'

'Didn't Pedro mind us borrowing them?'

'Don't know. Never asked him. He would've refused if I'd said anything, so I didn't bother. The more questions you ask Pedro, the less likely you are to have a job at the end of the week and there aren't many jobs going, so I keep my thoughts to myself. Better you should make use of them than them just sitting in the old shed doing nothing.'

'Thanks, Rafa. I really appreciate it. As you know, business has been terrible and I couldn't have afforded to buy any equipment. I'll let you have the rods and reels back as soon as I've cleared all the debts and can see a way forward.'

'No need to do that, Felix. Don't waste your money. Pedro won't ever use them again. If he ever notices they've gone, I'll tell him I took them home to repair them and send you word to get them back to me.'

'That's very good of you, Rafa. But don't go getting into trouble on my account!'

'No worries. I can't see Pedro wanting them again. He's too busy doing other things.'

'What does he get up to these days then, Rafa?'

'Don't ask me no questions and I'll tell you no lies!' quoted Rafa, staring somewhat sadly at his half empty glass.

'Fair enough! Just be careful, won't you?'

'Don't worry. I watch my back all the time. I'm sorry to say it, but I don't trust Pedro one centimetre. Sorry, I shouldn't say that about your brother, but I do wish I were working for you and not Pedro.'

'Yes, we would make a good team and I'd love to take you on one day, if I could. I'm sorry you had to sell up. I wish I could have helped you more then and could help you more now, Rafa.'

'You can. Just make sure your Sandro stays well away from Pedro. I was really worried that Pedro would persuade him to go into the business with him. I did think about having a quiet word with Sandro, but he might have thought it was just sour grapes from me to protect my job. These young'uns often do the opposite of what you say, don't they?'

'Yes, they do. You're right. It would probably have been counter-productive. But thanks for thinking of it.'

'Anyway, Pedro followed him about for weeks, trying to catch him every time he came off shift when he was working as a life-guard. He thought if he kept on about it, then Sandro would just give in for peace and quiet. I think the plan back-fired though, because your Sandro got really annoyed about being ambushed every day and lost his temper one afternoon and told his Uncle Pedro in no uncertain terms to leave him well and truly alone.'

'Thank goodness! We were very relieved, too. We don't trust Pedro either, as you know and we certainly didn't want Sandro working with him.'

'He's a fine lad, your Sandro. I think Pedro underestimated him. He's been in an absolutely foul mood since Sandro turned him down. Even more bitter and resentful and unpleasant than usual, if that's possible!'

'At least you've still got your job, Rafa.'

'Oh, I wasn't worried about Sandro from that point of view. I don't care about the job. In fact I hate the job. I just didn't want your Sandro mixed up with . . . .'

Rafa's voice trailed off and he gulped down some beer in embarrassment.

'I understand, Rafa. No need to say anything more. Just thanks again for everything. I won't forget it. I just wish you didn't have to work for Pedro. Meanwhile, would you like another beer? You've definitely earned it!'

As they walked slowly back to the car, hand in hand, Ana suddenly thought of the emails.

'Satya, you remember I downloaded those emails on to my own computer because I hadn't had time at work to check them?'

'Yes, Ana. Were any of them relevant to the conferences?'

'I don't think so, Satya. It was all medical stuff that I didn't understand. There were also some emails from an Indian girl trying to trace her father. Apparently he had been working as a surgeon at that new Clinic near the airport in Tenerife up until about three weeks ago and no-one has heard from him since. That's quite sad, isn't it?'

'I expect he'll turn up soon. He probably decided to do some sightseeing, before he went back to India and didn't bother to tell anyone.'

'I hope you're right. I know how I'd feel, if I lost my Dad.'

On the way home after spending a very pleasant hour with Rafa, Felix spotted Sandro outside the supermarket and walked over to him.

'I've got a little job for you later on, Sandro, if you wouldn't mind. It looks like a mathematical puzzle and Ana suggested you would be the one to crack it.'

'I'm flattered, Dad, that she thinks I'd be any good at that, but I'll be glad to have a try. See you later on! I'm just meeting up with Auntie Sara's boys. They wanted to tell me all about their hiking trip.'

'Okay! Remember me to them, won't you? You don't have to call her Auntie Sara now that you are older. She's not your real auntie!'

'I know I don't, Dad, but it seems more respectful and I've always called her that.'

'Okay, Sandro, I appreciate that. Have fun! See you later!'

Chano grinned as he looked at the text which Felix had sent him. Felix had warned him he found mobile phones difficult! There were several letters in the wrong place and some odd punctuation, but he understood the gist of it. If his friend, Alfredo, was on shift today, he was sure he wouldn't mind looking through all the passenger lists for the last three or four weeks to see if Karthik Nayar, the Indian surgeon, had flown out of either airport on Tenerife. The information was supposedly confidential but this was all in a good cause and he knew that Alfredo would agree. Chano was only too pleased to help Felix and his daughter, if he could. He was a very likeable chap and he had enjoyed passing the time with him down at the harbour that morning. He wondered idly how old his daughter was, but decided he ought to concentrate on the matter in hand. So he quickly composed a text to his friend, asking him for the relevant information and promising to take him out for a beer the following week. Things were definitely improving. He felt much healthier and happier after his short holiday, despite the untoward events of the last day. He was looking forward to having a drink with Felix one day soon and finding out more about squid and fishing in general. He had a whole day off tomorrow. He had planned to spend it with his girlfriend but she had become increasingly fed-up with his antisocial working hours and he had been unable to persuade her to stick around. Never mind! Just imagine! A whole day with no passengers, no luggage and very definitely no squid!

'Hi Mum! What's for tea? When will it be ready?'

'Sandro, do you ever think of anything else except your stomach?' asked Maria. 'Tea will be served in exactly 33 minutes when the fish pie has cooked. Would you like to make yourself useful by laying up the table and putting out some water and juice?'

'Will do, Mum. By the way, Dad mentioned some puzzle he wanted me to try to solve.'

'Oh yes! The piece of paper is on the desk under the dictionary. Please lay the table first for me, Sandro, before you get engrossed in your detective work.'

'Of course, mother dear! Would I dare do anything else?'

Sandro deftly dodged the tea-towel, which his mother aimed playfully at him, fetched the cutlery and crockery and laid the table in record time. He wiped four glasses and put them by each table setting and put the jugs by the sink to remind himself to fill them up before they sat down to their meal that evening. He then retrieved the paper with the coded email and stretched out comfortably on the settee with a pad and pencil. This was going to be a tough one to crack. He had no idea what any of the symbols related to and was still waiting for some sort of inspiration when Felix and Ana arrived back home.

'Hi Mum!' said Ana happily as she entered the kitchen. 'Something smells wonderful!'

'Could be your Mum's perfume or it might just be that fish pie in the oven,' said her Dad, giving his wife and daughter an affectionate hug.

'I'm about ready to dish up, if you could persuade Sandro to abandon his enigma code and put the drinks on the table.'

'I'll do the drinks, Mum. Would you like to fetch your mathematical genius, Dad?'

Eventually they were all seated at the table and Maria served out the pie. They helped themselves to salad. Conversation was sparse while they ate the delicious meal.

Everyone had second helpings except Ana. Sandro couldn't resist teasing her that her appetite was waning because she was in love.

'Don't be ridiculous, Sandro,' snapped Ana.

'Ah! Methinks the lady doth protest too much!' retorted Sandro, totally unabashed.

'How was the lizard-hunting, Ana?' enquired her mother innocently.

Ana immediately started laughing and then managed to splutter an explanation of lizard-hunting for the benefit of her father and brother.

'They didn't call it that in our day,' said Felix. 'I think your Mum would have run a mile, if I'd suggested lizard-hunting! You know how she hates creepy-crawlies of any sort.'

Uproarious laughter followed this remark and the meal continued merrily. Then Maria winked at her daughter and asked her if the research team working for the Centre had seen any of these elusive creatures when they had been out lizard-hunting. Eventually Ana's laughter subsided and she was able to reply:

'No, no-one has seen any for nearly three months now. It's rather worrying.'

'That will give you plenty of excuses for more lizard-hunting then,' said her brother.

Ana ignored him and the innuendo, as she continued:

'Actually, the two research assistants did discover something strange. They've been surveying the cliffs near La Rajita, because that's where some of the lizards were last sighted and of course the research assistants have had to be camouflaged and keep well out of sight in order to observe the lizards, should they deign to appear. While they had the cliffs under surveillance, they were amazed to find that the village was not as deserted as they had been told.'

'Don't tell me,' interjected Sandro, barely able to speak for laughing, 'that the lizards have invaded the village and are living a life of sheer luxury in that derelict old fish factory instead of being perched uncomfortably on some narrow cliff ledge.'

'I don't think so somehow,' replied Ana, trying to be serious. 'I think the researchers just wondered what was going on at the fish factory down by the shore, because every day two men in a battered old vehicle drove past their hiding-place by the cliffs up to the main road and returned two and a half hours later. Lizards don't come out of the crevices until the air warms up, so the research assistants only arrived mid-morning and left late afternoon so they never saw the men arrive or leave.'

'Perhaps the two strangers are hippies and are living in the factory. It's shabby on the outside but I expect it is still weatherproof,' suggested Felix.

'Did Satya's colleagues have any idea what the men were doing?' asked Maria.

'No, not really. They said in the report they wrote for Satya that they could hear a motor humming, perhaps a generator but otherwise there was no clue as to what the men were up to. They could have had anything stashed in that van as well. We were joking that they were printing counterfeit money.'

'I hope it's nothing to do with Pedro,' said Felix, alarm apparent in his voice.

'Dad, you've just reminded me! When I took Satya to La Rajita sightseeing the first time, we saw Uncle Pedro's old truck at the end of the track down on the beach. Uncle wasn't there though. It was Rafa, who was unloading crates from the truck.'

'Oh! That's okay, then. Rafa must have been taking fish and other supplies to them. Perhaps they are trying to get the factory going again.'

'I shouldn't think it was a viable proposition now. There are too many EU regulations and all sorts of Health and Safety issues now to contend with,' said Maria thoughtfully.

'Since when did Uncle Pedro ever worry about rules and regulations?' asked Sandro. 'He'd find a way to circumvent anyone or anything that stood in his path,' he added rather bitterly.

'Well,' said Maria, trying to be conciliatory. 'As long as none of us is involved, then it is up to Uncle Pedro and his conscience what he gets mixed up with. The less we know about his business dealings, the better.'

'What's for afters, Mum?'

'You and your stomach, Sandro! Well, I've made a chocolate cake or there's plenty of fruit, if you'd prefer.'

'No contest, mother dear, chocolate cake it must be! I have to nourish my sweet brain cells or I'll never crack that code.'

'You're impossible, Sandro! Make sure you leave some for the rest of us!'

Maria returned the floor polisher into its cramped cupboard for the night and made her way rather wearily to the main door. She let herself out quietly, checked that the door locked behind her and headed for home. She was half-way home when she remembered the mobile phone she had found in the cloakroom. She had intended to hand it into the Security staff on her way out, but it had slipped her mind, because no-one was at the desk when she left. Oh well, she thought to herself, it will keep until tomorrow. Ana could hand it in to Security in the morning. She certainly didn't have the energy or the inclination to traipse back there now. All she wanted to do now was go home. Satya had not been working tonight, so she had not spoken to a soul during her lonely shift.

She smiled to herself, as she thought about him lizard-hunting with Ana. Who would have thought that lizard-hunting could make them so happy! She was so glad that the job had worked out for Ana. Satya was a good friend and had taken care of her daughter from the very first day and allayed Maria's worst fears and misgivings about working for the Professor. And they were enjoying each other's company so much. She had never seen Satya so cheerful and relaxed and Ana was positively in seventh heaven. Ana was well aware that the job could end at any moment but had sensibly decided to make the most of it while she could. She was saving every euro she earned and putting it in a special account for university later. She was a daughter to be proud of and Maria would miss her terribly, when she flew the nest eventually, as fly she must. They were the best of friends, very similar in temperament, had always confided in each other and had fun together. Maria felt very blessed.

Jeevan struggled up the uneven path near the cliff, skirted round the edge of the forest and reached one of the wooden research huts just in time for a late lunch break. Not a single lizard in sight so far this morning. Where were they all hiding? Frustrating beasties! Admittedly, it was still rather overcast and the canny creatures liked brilliant sunshine. Perhaps they would appear in the afternoon under the forecast clear blue skies. He had reluctantly left the shrewd reptiles to his colleague, Amit, for the rest of the day's surveillance work. Jeevan intended to spend the afternoon quietly updating his paperwork for Satya. First of all, however, he decided that he would have a short siesta in the hut. He opened the door rather absent-mindedly and then froze on the threshold.

Back home Sandro was sprawled untidily on the settee, concentrating hard on the paper in his hand.

He was scribbling on the pad and crossing things out, apparently completely absorbed in the task, when Maria came back after her cleaning shift. He took her totally by surprise when he suddenly spoke to her.

'Hi Mum! Would you like a cup of coffee or something stronger? Or can I tempt you with an extremely delicious chocolate sponge cake made by a reputable chef in the vicinity?'

'Coffee and a piece of my own cake would be lovely, thanks Sandro.'

'Your wish is my command. Please rest your weary old bones and I will bring it to you.'

'Less of the old bones, please Sandro!' quipped his Mum, sinking gratefully into the old armchair, as her son uncoiled himself athletically from the settee.

'Have you made any headway with the great enigma?' asked Maria.

'I've unscrambled times and dates on one section. I just have no idea at the moment what the rest refers to. Have a look at it, Mum, and see if it means anything to you.'

'I will later on, Sandro, if that's okay. I'm just exhausted after my shift. Added to which, it's very humid tonight. It's probably brewing up for a thunderstorm. It was really hot and sticky coming back from the Centre. Just for the moment if you don't mind, I'd like to sit here and do absolutely nothing and be thoroughly pampered.'

'That can be arranged, Mother dear. Just relax those old bones of yours and waiter service will arrive shortly with coffee and cake for your delectation.'

'Don't push it too far, young man! I might be too tired at the moment to chuck a cushion at you, but I have a long and reliable memory.'

Sandro grinned widely as he headed towards the kitchen. He had such a wonderful family, he reflected. How lucky was he!

Felix was walking back up from the harbour when his mobile rang. He was expecting a call from Juan, but was surprised to find that it was the pilot, Chano, who was on the phone. They had a long friendly chat and Felix learned that Chano had nine hours to spare the next day in between flights. Felix, Sandro and Maria were not working either tomorrow, so the timing could not have been better. He immediately invited Chano for lunch with the family and offered to meet him at the bus stop at 1000hrs. Felix headed home, pleasantly anticipating spending time with the family and his new-found friend. He knew Maria would love to meet him and would be only too happy to provide lunch. She was always very hospitable and loved company.

'Thanks, Sandro. That was very welcome. You're quite domesticated really, aren't you! I must have taught you something after all.'

'Don't push it too far, Mother dear, or I may have to chuck a cushion in your direction! Seriously though, I was just saying to Dad that making us speak English at home has proved to be invaluable. That's down to you, Mum, and I can't thank you enough. I know I've grumbled and groaned about it for years, but it was one of the best things you could have done for us and I'm sorry if I was such a pain.'

'Thank you, Sandro. That means a lot. Many times I thought it wasn't worth the hassle and aggravation and it would just be easier to give up the idea and speak Spanish at home together. Dad and I wanted you both to be bi-lingual and Dad wanted to keep up his English, too. We still harboured our dream of running a family business one day connected with tourism and we knew that English was essential for that.'

'Perhaps you and Dad will realise your dream one day, Mum, before your bones get too old, I hope.'

'If you mention 'old bones' again, young Sandro, you'll have more than a cushion chucked at you!'

'Okay, Mum! Truce! I promise, for the moment . . . . at least!'

'Changing the subject, you infuriating young man, how did Sara's boys get on?'

'Oh! They had a great time hiking with their two mates. They all want to do it again for longer and camp out under the stars. I had the impression that Auntie Sara was not too impressed by that idea.'

'I expect she'll come round to it. It's always scary when your children want to be more adventurous and go off on their own. Look at all my grey hairs!'

'You've stood the trials and tribulations of bringing us up quite well, Mum. I can't see any grey hairs, not from this distance anyway!'

'Thank you for that back-handed compliment. I'll treasure it in my old age. Where did Sara's boys go?'

'Up to Garajonay by bus, then they trekked through the forest up to the top of Mount Garajonay and then headed off to the west and ended up near Chipude. Then they scrambled half-way down that deep ravine towards La Dama. They intended going down to the beach for a swim but there was thick smoke coming from a big bonfire nearby so they didn't fancy it and decided to head back up to the main road instead. They eventually found a way-marked route to Alajero, where they stopped for a rest and a bite to eat and eventually caught the last bus back to here. Auntie Sara was very relieved to see them back in one piece. She shouldn't worry so much; they're very sensible boys. They really enjoyed the adventure and can't wait to do it again.'

'You always worry about your children, Sandro, even when they're grown up. It's all part of the joys and sorrows of being a parent.'

'I hope there will be more joys than sorrows for you in the future, Mum. I know I've been pretty stubborn and stupid at times and I'm so sorry but hopefully that's all in the past. I'll make it up to you, I promise.'

Some time later Felix arrived home and told them about Chano, the charter plane pilot.

'I hope you invited him here to lunch,' said Maria generously.

'Yes, I did. I hoped you would be happy with that. I don't take you for granted, Maria, but I know we are all off work tomorrow, except Ana, of course and I thought you would enjoy having a new face around the table.'

'That would be lovely, Felix. I'll cook something easy and we can all spend more time talking together. Will that be all right?'

'Sounds an excellent idea. We don't want you stuck in the kitchen slaving over a hot stove when you should be enjoying yourself. We'll all help with the meal; that's only fair. It's your day off as well.'

'Thanks, Felix. I wonder if Ana and Satya could slip out for an hour and join us? I must remember to give Ana this mobile to hand in to Lost Property. I found it in the cloakroom, but the security desk wasn't manned when I left, so I forgot about it. I must be getting old, if I'm forgetting things like that. Sara and I were only talking about that the other day. My memory is certainly not what it was!'

'You're tired, Mum, that's all. I know I was teasing you earlier about your old bones, but you aren't old and there's nothing at all wrong with your memory. It's vastly superior to mine! So please don't worry about it.'

'Thanks for that vote of confidence, Sandro. It's much appreciated.'

'Shall I have a look at the phone and see if I can discover whose it is?'

'Yes, if you want. The keypad is probably locked and we'll just have to wait until someone comes forward to claim it. Anyway, have a try, if you want to,' said Maria, handing the phone over to Sandro. 'You're becoming quite a puzzle-solver, aren't you?'

Rafa's mobile sparked into life to announce that the dreaded Pedro was calling. With a sigh of resignation Rafa picked up the phone and listened to the nasty bullying voice.

'I need you to work late on Thursday night, Rafa. Whatever you had planned, cancel it. This takes absolute priority and I won't take 'no' for an answer,' threatened Pedro.

'Okay,' agreed Rafa, somewhat reluctantly. 'Usual time down at the boat?'

'Yes, and don't dare be even one minute late or you know what will happen!'

A click signalled the end of yet another unpleasant exchange, as Pedro abruptly switched off his mobile. It was never he, Rafa, who was late; it was always Pedro who turned up thirty minutes or more after the agreed time and he had usually been drinking heavily. Rafa always expected Pedro to be violently sick when they were out at sea, but his stomach seemed to be made of iron, like the rest of him. He wished he could escape from Pedro and this awful racket. He hated every minute of it, but he couldn't work out how to get away from all of it, Pedro included, whilst still remaining alive and healthy. He was only too aware that he couldn't do it on his own, but he didn't want to involve anyone else and endanger their lives too.

'Did you get anywhere with that code, Sandro?' asked Felix, making himself comfortable on the old sofa. 'It has defeated me, though I hate to admit it.'

'Not very far,' replied Sandro. 'I think that the digits at the end of each line represent times and dates. The letters I assume must be people, but without specific clues, it's virtually impossible to work out who they might be. Have a look at the bits I've transcribed and see if it triggers any thoughts. You too, Mum, if your 'old bones' will make it to the sofa beside Dad.'

'Don't mention my 'old bones' again, Sandro! I'm far too tired to retaliate and I cannot be held responsible for my actions!' She went over and collected the piece of paper and the pad from Sandro and sat down beside Felix, smiling contentedly. 'Besides,' she continued, 'you can't really take advantage of your dear old mother, can you Sandro?'

Maria studied the piece of paper and the pad where Sandro had written possible ideas.

Felix put his arm round her and tried to concentrate on the cryptic messages.

CP + D + NODE +7FC > TFN 19301704

Sandro had written @ 1930 hrs on 17th April

P + R + 10AB > LAR 22301704

If Sandro was right, then 'P' and 'R' were meeting with someone at 'LAR' at 2230 hrs on 17th April

CP + D + 14DE > PDS 09452004	0945 hrs on 20th April
CP + C + NODE + 7EC > PDS 09452304	0945 hrs on 23rd April
CP + C +6DE + 7EC > PDS 08300305	0830 hrs on 3rd May
P + R + 10AB > LAR 21450305	2145 hrs on 3rd May
CP + C + 10DE > TFN 14300305	1430 hrs on 3rd May

'I have a strange gut feeling,' said Maria, 'that P might stand for Pedro and R for poor Rafa and I shudder to think what they might have been doing so late on the 17th April and again on the 3rd of May.'

'Mum, you're a genius. I know what they were doing. They were out in the boat. I saw them coming back into the harbour when I was having a drink with Martin a couple of nights ago. They didn't unload anything on to the quay, so they hadn't been fishing. I thought it was very odd at the time. Uncle Pedro was up to something illegal, I'm sure.'

'Ana saw Rafa at La Rajita the other day, didn't she? What if LAR stood for La Rajita?'

So who or what were the '10AB', they all wondered.

Sandro was still fiddling with the mobile phone his mother had found in the Conference Centre when he suddenly almost fell off the chair in his excitement as he shouted out:

'Done it! I know whose phone this is and I recognise some of the numbers he's been calling, though I don't understand why.'

'I hope you are not developing criminal tendencies, Sandro. You seem to be getting rather too good at cracking codes.' Felix laughed good-naturedly.

'Don't keep us in suspense, Sandro!' pleaded his mother. 'Whose phone is it?'

Their footsteps crunched on the coarse black sand, as they walked hand in hand in the moonlight. It was very peaceful away from the night-life by the harbour promenade. The waves plopped quietly on to the beach and gently splashed the nearby rocks. Satya took Ana gently in his arms and kissed her softly. Ana responded willingly and then put her head lovingly on his shoulder.

'You are beautiful, Ana, with your long black silky hair and soft sun-tanned skin.'

'You make me sound like an advertisement for shampoo or skin cream!'

'Sorry,' replied Satya, laughing. 'I am being serious! You are truly beautiful.'

They stood together on the shore, totally in harmony with each other and with nature. Ana could have cried with happiness. She would treasure this golden moment for ever. She had found her soul-mate in the most unlikely of circumstances. Satya called it 'fate' and he, too, could not have been happier. Who said romance was dead! They stood there in the moonlight together, listening to the gentle waves and gazing lovingly into each other's eyes. They held on to the magic and romance for a while longer, before they headed rather reluctantly up the beach towards the road and Ana's home. Work tomorrow unfortunately! Reality called!

Sandro waved the mobile phone triumphantly. He was surprised at what he had discovered and could barely wait to tell his parents.

'You won't believe this, Mum! The phone belongs to your weasel Professor and he has been quite clever in trying to delete information.'

'Obviously not clever enough,' remarked his father drily, 'to prevent you gaining access.'

'It was fun,' said Sandro. 'I'm discovering new techniques all the time. It stirs up my brain cells and it's really very interesting.'

'Come on, Sandro! Spill the beans! Who has the Professor been contacting?' asked Maria. 'Actually, I'm not sure we should be prying into his private affairs. I only wanted to know whose phone it was.'

'So did I!' replied Sandro. 'But I can't resist a challenge and just had to puzzle it out.'

'Fair enough! I'll forgive you! I'm dying of curiosity too. So tell us more!'

At that moment a blissfully happy Ana arrived home and came into the sitting-room. Her parents were looking expectantly at Sandro and she wondered what was going on. Her brother was grinning and staring at a mobile phone which she did not recognise.

'Have I interrupted something important?' Ana was somewhat disconcerted.

'I'll say,' quipped Sandro. 'Mum found this phone at work and I volunteered to find out who it belonged to and I have. Luckily the owner hadn't locked the keypad so it was easy to hack into. It's the Professor's phone and he has some very weird contacts. I was just about to tell Mum and Dad, when you came in.'

'Sorry,' said Ana. 'Please do continue, Sandro!'

'Okay, sis! I bet this will surprise you all. The four numbers which I recognised easily are: Satya, the Conference Hotel, where Uncle Juan works, Uncle Pedro and that new Clinic near the airport in Tenerife. I only recognised that one because Antonio gave me his work number as well as his mobile number, because his phone was on the blink. I just texted Satya to ask him if he recognised the number of the phone you found and he confirmed it was the Professor's. The Professor has also been called several times from Africa and he has sent loads of loving texts to someone called 'C'. Somehow, I never thought that miserable creep would have a love life!'

Silence followed while they all digested these peculiar revelations.

Jeevan was rooted to the spot in surprise. Someone was obviously living in the hut. Things had been moved. Two bottles of water from the emergency supply they always kept there had been emptied. The wooden chair was over at the far side well away from the desk, presumably to make room for the makeshift pillow of palm leaves on the floor. Who was desperate enough to want to stay in this rickety old shed? Either they had now moved on or they had no belongings. Jeevan went outside and surveyed the area around the hut. No sign of anyone or anything else untoward. He knew that none of the research team had been to the hut for three days. It was therefore entirely possible that someone had made this their temporary home. How strange! Not an urgent problem, but it had dispelled all thoughts of a quiet afternoon siesta! With a sigh of resignation he shouldered his rucksack, closed the door of the hut and headed off in the direction of the main road.

※

'What could possibly connect the Professor and Uncle Pedro?' asked Felix in surprise.

'What could possibly connect the Professor and the Clinic in Tenerife?' asked Ana.

'By the way, Ana, talking about clinics just reminded me,' said Felix. 'That charter pilot, Chano, called in a favour from a friend at Passport Control in Tenerife and he kindly went through all the flight schedules and other relevant information and discovered that the Indian surgeon, Karthik, that you were trying to trace, hasn't left the Canary Islands on any flight.'

'Thanks, Dad, for finding that out. I'll email his daughter. He must still be somewhere in the Islands. Perhaps Satya is right; he has just gone sight-seeing without telling anyone and is alive and well. I hope so.'

'What did you just say, Felix?' asked Maria in dismay.

'Ana asked me to find out if this Indian girl's father, Karthik Nayar, had gone back to India. He was working at the new Clinic near the airport in Tenerife and disappeared off the radar about three weeks ago. I asked the pilot, Chano, who is coming to lunch tomorrow, if he could find out unofficially from the passenger lists whether he had left Tenerife from either Los Rodeos or Reina Sofia airport and he hasn't left yet.'

'Oh! No! No! This is terrible! It cannot be true. It must not be true. I feel really sick.'

They stared in horror, as a deathly pale Maria rushed out of the room.

Rafa was slumped over his kitchen table. He looked bleary-eyed and miserable, as though he had been drinking heavily. In fact, he hadn't touched a drop. He knew that if he started, he might never stop. He never had more than two beers at a time in case the alcohol loosened his tongue because that could well have dire consequences for him.

He couldn't go on like this. He just couldn't. Somehow he must extricate himself from this mess. Should he go to the police? No point. They probably wouldn't believe his unlikely account. Even if they did, they probably wouldn't act quickly enough to keep him alive. He would be implicated and Pedro would make sure that he never lived to tell the tale. What a mess! Why did he ever borrow money from Pedro? How utterly stupid! Isobel's medical care had been so expensive. They had tried everything, but to no avail. What else could he have done? He would have done anything to save his wife. His thoughts had been going round his head in circles for hours now. There was no solution. He felt like the waking dead, wandering around like a battered zombie. If he couldn't clear his conscience, he couldn't sleep properly. If he couldn't sleep properly, then sooner or later he might inadvertently say something incriminating. That could well prove fatal. Whatever he did, it seemed to him, he would end up dead and that particular prospect had little appeal.

'Mum, come and sit down. Have a sip of water! Whatever's wrong?'

Ana was very worried as she fussed round her mother. She had never seen her like this before. Slowly some colour came back into Maria's cheeks, as she continued to sip the ice-cold water. Her breathing became easier. Felix put his arm round her to comfort her, while Sandro looked on, totally at a loss to know what to do in the circumstances. Eventually Maria recovered her equilibrium.

'Sorry to worry you all! It was just such a shock. I suddenly put the pieces of information together and realised what has been going on. I overheard the Professor shouting the other day about 'Karthik', but I thought it was a place. I think your surgeon is still alive and I have a shrewd idea where he might be.'

'Don't worry about that, Mum. Are you feeling better? You had us all worried,' said Sandro. 'You are never ill. You are the glue that keeps us all together.'

'Thanks, Sandro. I'm okay but I'm afraid that a lot of other people are in danger.'

'What do you mean, my darling? Take your time and please don't upset yourself!' Felix tried to comfort and reassure his wife.

Maria looked over to her son and said as steadily as she could:

'Sandro, before that mobile is handed back, could you copy all the contacts and the messages sent and any other data you manage to find. It is vital evidence and may be destroyed by the Professor as soon as he has the phone back. It is highly incriminating.'

'Yes, of course, Mum. That's easy. I'll download all the data now and print off copies for you. It won't take a minute.'

The tension in the room was palpable. All eyes were riveted on Sandro.

'All done, Mum! Two copies hot off the press!'

'Why can't we just hand the mobile over to the police if this is so serious?' queried Ana.

'Because we must not alert the Professor under any circumstances. Everything must seem normal until we have found the surgeon and brought him back here to safety, if we can manage that. We'll return the mobile to the Professor tomorrow morning somehow and with any luck he won't suspect a thing.'

Slumped in a tatty armchair in his tiny rented flat, Rafa had dozed uneasily for several hours. He was seriously agitated and his brain had reacted by lacing his sleep with horrendous nightmares. He had been cracked over the head with a baseball bat, thrown overboard and drowned out to sea. He had been shot at as he left the old factory and the tyre of the old truck had been punctured and he and the truck had careered off the rough track into a treacherous deep ravine where he had died in a fire-ball of diesel. In another scenario Pedro had strangled him, stuffed him in a crate and heaved him over the side of the trawler to feed the whales and dolphins off the coast by La Dama. In every nightmare he ended up dead. Dead. Dead. Dead. He stood up unsteadily and fetched a glass of water. He must get help. There were only two people to whom he could turn for advice. He would go and see them after breakfast.

Pedro stared gloomily at the bright lights dancing round the harbour bars and cafes. He sat alone, hunched over his drink. The more he drank, the more miserable he became. He had failed dismally in his plan to have Sandro working for him. Who would have thought that gutless youngster would have had the temerity to turn down a golden job with his uncle? Pedro had to have a Plan B. He must have revenge. Revenge for what? Pedro couldn't remember. He had everything already, hadn't he? He had 'stolen' his brother's house, his legacy. He had wrecked his business. He had tried to steal his wife, but he had been no match for the wrath and disgust of the feisty Maria. He had totally ignored his lovely niece, Ana. He had carefully groomed his nephew, Sandro, but all to no avail. He had all the money and power, but in reality he had nothing worthwhile. He was wretched, cantankerous and frequently very nasty. His brother, Felix now had no money, no business, no house of his own and yet he was happy and well-liked and respected. Where had it all gone wrong? In his drunken state Pedro could make no sense of this conundrum. There was only one solution to injustice like this. He ordered another beer and whisky chaser. His speech was now very slurred and the other customers decided it would be wise to avoid this brooding, evil hulk who seemed so disgruntled with life.

The family waited quietly until Maria felt able to explain what had caused her to have such a violent reaction earlier. Her breathing was still somewhat erratic and she was still pale.

'I don't quite know where to start. There are so many disparate elements in this story and it is only by pure chance that I have seen a connection. I hope I'm mistaken, but my gut instinct is that a terrible crime has been and probably still is being committed.'

'Just go slowly, Maria and explain bit by bit. I simply can't imagine what has upset you.'

'Would you rather leave it until tomorrow, Mum?' asked Ana solicitously.

'In some ways, yes, because you will all have a sleepless night when I explain. But I think I'd better tell you all now. I'm afraid that if I'm right, it is a really horrific tale.'

'Shall I cancel Chano coming to lunch tomorrow, Maria? I'm sure he won't mind.'

'No! No! Don't do that! I think he can fill in the bits of the jigsaw that are missing. You said he was a decent chap. I'm sure he will be happy to help solve the mystery.'

'He did say he had a lot to tell me. Said he'd had one hell of a frightening adventure with his co-pilot, Domingo and wanted to run it past me.'

'This is becoming more and more complicated,' said Ana. 'I haven't a clue what's going on or why. Please enlighten me, Mum. I'm getting quite worried.'

'Well, I was chatting with Satya one evening when he was working late. He was extremely annoyed because the Professor seemed to have no interest whatsoever in the various research projects which Satya was co-ordinating and he just couldn't understand it. Now I realise why. The fact is: the Centre is just a front for the Professor's other activities, so obviously he couldn't care less about the biodiversity of the Islands or conservation or green energy sources. The whole thing is a dreadful scam. I always thought that the Professor was a weirdo.'

'Go on, Mum. What are these other activities that the Professor is so involved in?' Sandro asked, looking very puzzled.

'Those emails you decoded, Felix. I was intrigued as to what all the medical terms meant and I looked them all up on the internet. It was just an intellectual exercise then to satisfy my curiosity, but I realised suddenly this evening the significance of what I had discovered. Those emails were about people with diabetes who had kidney failure; people who needed corneal transplants to avert blindness; people who were HIV positive who needed several different organs—what was termed 'multivisceral transplants'; steroids to prevent the rejection of transplanted organs; special techniques for storing donated organs for much longer periods than heretofore; anaesthesia research and various therapies to prevent infection and rejection of transplanted organs.'

Maria paused in her explanation. The family sat transfixed by the gory revelations.

Suddenly Ana broke the silence as realization dawned on her.

'The Clinic in Tenerife, where that Indian girl's father, Karthik, was working. Antonio said he left suddenly after a bust-up about 'incompatibility.' The surgeon, Karthik, didn't leave the Clinic because of a clash of personalities as we innocently assumed. He left because the donor organs he was supposed to transplant were incompatible with the recipients and were therefore highly likely to be rejected. He obviously didn't want to proceed with the operations on that unethical basis. So he was probably sacked. If the car that took him away didn't take him to the airport, where did it go? Is the poor Indian surgeon still alive?'

'I think he may still be alive, but he is in great danger. I think he came across from Tenerife to La Gomera on the ferry under duress and is now a prisoner at the old fish factory at La Rajita. I think he is being kept under guard there by the men that Satya's research assistants accidentally had under surveillance, when they were trying to catch a glimpse of the giant lizards.'

Maria recounted the gist of what Sara had told her about the six Indian guests arriving unexpectedly and then two desperately ill guests being carted off unceremoniously in a white van from the rear entrance of the hotel in the early hours of the morning. That in turn linked in with the Professor's peculiar tirade on the telephone about 'taking them back to Karthik', which she had not understood at the time, since she had never heard the name of the Indian surgeon mentioned and had incorrectly assumed that 'Karthik' was a place.

'Chano, the pilot, was telling me that he had flown six Indian passengers over one morning and two of them looked awfully ill,' interjected Felix.

'So some of the transplants obviously went badly wrong because the transplanted organs were in poor condition or not compatible,' mused Ana. 'The Clinic in Tenerife would not want any failures on its records so the sick patients were quietly flown over here and transferred to the Conference Hotel but they couldn't fetch medical help for them at the Hotel, because too many awkward questions would have been asked. So they took them surreptitiously to Karthik at the old fish factory for him to try to sort them out. That's why Jeevan and Amit could hear machinery running there.'

'Where does Pedro fit into this conspiracy, Maria?'
'I'm not entirely sure yet. I'm still working it out. Anyway, it's getting late and we'd better get some sleep.

Ana, it is absolutely essential that you act normally tomorrow. Don't hand the mobile into security. Can you ask Satya to leave it in the Gentlemen's Cloakroom? The Professor will find it there when he comes in and will suspect nothing. Keep track of the Professor all day, if you can. Text us at once if he goes out at lunchtime. Keep him busy in the building if you can. Stay indoors with Satya. Don't come back for lunch, much as I would like you both to come. If there are any problems, let us know at once. It's really important. It might be a matter of life and death.'

'Okay, Mum. Will do. I'm not sure any of us will sleep much tonight now that we have a fair idea of what is going on.'

'Probably not, but we have to try. There's a lot to be done tomorrow.'

Ana and Sandro trooped off upstairs to their respective rooms. Felix and Maria sat huddled together on the sofa in stunned silence, their thoughts in turmoil. They were both beginning to think the unthinkable.

Next morning Maria and Felix were clearing up the breakfast clutter. Ana had already left for work, having assured herself that her mother was well. Sandro had escaped to the sitting-room to try to work out the last of the code. There was an urgent knocking on the front door of the cottage and Felix went off to investigate.

'Good to see you, Rafa! Come on in! Make yourself at home! What can we do for you this bright and sunny morning?'

Felix ushered Rafa into the kitchen, where Maria smiled at him and asked if he would like a coffee or anything to eat.

'I'm sorry to trouble you all. I'd love a coffee, please. You are both always so welcoming. Thank you.'

'No trouble at all, Rafa. If you don't mind me saying so, you don't look at all well. I'll make some more coffee and you can sit down comfortably and tell us what's wrong.'

Five minutes later Rafa gratefully accepted the cup of coffee from Maria and relaxed a little in their cosy companionable kitchen.

'I don't know where to start,' stuttered Rafa. 'I'm in a terrible mess. I can't get out of it by myself, but I don't want to involve anyone else, because it could get them in trouble. You are the only real friends I have and the last thing I want is to endanger your lives.'

'Let us be the judge of that, Rafa! You clearly can't go on as you are. You seem terrified of someone or something. You've always been a good friend to us and we can't have you worried to death. We will help you all we can.'

Felix reached across the kitchen table and took Rafa's hands in his own. Rafa was so moved that two lonely tears escaped from the corners of his eyes and dripped slowly down his cheeks. He blinked rapidly and blushed furiously.

Maria spoke quickly to cover up any embarrassment he might feel.

'Would we be right in assuming that Pedro is involved and La Rajita?'

Rafa was clearly disconcerted by her question but also relieved that his friends were aware of at least some of the facts.

'Yes, it is,' confirmed Rafa. 'I don't know exactly what's going on, but it's a nasty racket. Pedro blackmailed me into it, because I stupidly borrowed money off him to pay for all those expensive treatments for Isobel. I can't just leave, because now I know too much and Pedro would have no qualms about killing me, if I tried to get out. He makes a lot of money out of this little venture and he's not about to give that up in a hurry. I don't know what to do. I know I'm totally expendable. Whichever way I try to escape from Pedro, I end up dead. If I disappeared, Pedro would just replace me with another victim. That's why I didn't want your Sandro involved.'

Back at the Conference Centre Satya was just returning to his office when the Professor accosted him, rather anxiously.

'Have you by any chance seen my mobile phone, Satya?'

'There's one on the windowsill in the cloakroom. I don't know if that's yours, Sir. I noticed it earlier but decided to wait until lunchtime before handing it over to Security, in case the owner turned up to reclaim it.'

'Thank you so much, Satya. I expect it's mine. I must be getting absent-minded in my old age! I shall be in the office all day, if you need me. I have tons of paperwork to do!'

Pleasantly surprised by the Professor's unusual politeness, Satya winked conspiratorially at Ana. The Professor was 'in' all day, so that was another problem solved.

The terrible tension seemed to seep away as Rafa relaxed in the homely cottage kitchen. He was drinking his second coffee and enjoying a piece of chocolate cake which Maria had kindly offered him. He wished he could stay here forever in this kind caring home, a million miles away from the callousness of his employer and blackmailer.

'I hear you have been feeding my squid at La Dama,' laughed Felix, hoping to lighten the atmosphere. 'I couldn't understand why they had deserted my fishing grounds!'

'Sorry about that, Felix! I hate the very sight of squid now. I'll tell them to go back, if you like. I'll even give you some mackerel to keep them happy!' Rafa grinned back.

Just then Sandro came into the kitchen, saw Rafa and greeted him warmly.

'Rafa, do tell me! I'm really curious. Why were you coming back into the harbour so late the other night? I was having a beer with my friend, Martin, at that new bar on the harbour promenade, so I saw you and Uncle Pedro clearly and you didn't unload anything on to the quay, so I don't think you had been fishing.'

Rafa looked very uncomfortable and squirmed in embarrassment.

'It's all right, Rafa. Sandro knows as much as we know. We were working it all out together last night. There are still bits of the jigsaw missing, but we're getting there.'

Rafa sighed, looking very dejected. Eventually he plucked up the courage to say:

'Every so often we rendezvous about two hours out to sea with a boatload of Africans. An ocean-going yacht has brought them close to the rendezvous point and then transferred them into a small open boat. Each time we are only allowed to take a specific number and the remaining Africans face almost certain death in their leaky old boat which is anything but seaworthy. I hate it when we have to leave them behind, but perhaps they are in fact the lucky ones. We take the others to La Rajita. I give them food and water on the way, even though Pedro objects strongly and threatens me with dire reprisals every time. I don't care any more what he thinks. Those poor Africans all look so forlorn. They own nothing but the rags on their backs. Yet they are so grateful to be rescued and given food and water. They must think they are going to be safe and start a new life here on La Gomera, far away from the death and destruction they have left behind them in Africa. I feel terrible every time I think about it, but I don't know what to do to stop it.'

Rafa stopped talking, obviously very upset and emotional.

'Rafa, what happens to the Africans at La Rajita?' asked Maria gently.

'I don't know, Maria. I really don't. I assumed it was some sort of sex-trafficking or a modern version of the slave trade. I really don't know. I never ask any questions. I know that's cowardly, but it is a valid self-preservation technique, where Pedro is in the equation. Pedro hates the Africans, so I don't think they are being taken to a five star hotel. I had to take seven crates of squid over to La Rajita the other day. I've never been down there before. Pedro had to go to Tenerife unexpectedly and couldn't do the delivery, so he told me to do it. Two men met me outside the derelict factory. They were even more uncouth and rough than Pedro and I was very glad to get out of there and back to civilization. There was no sign of the Africans or anyone else, so perhaps they had been moved on somewhere else. I was so relieved they weren't there. I have been having nightmares about what might be happening at that old factory. I just don't know what goes on there. I have no idea either what the men wanted with the squid and I definitely didn't ask. A friendly chat with those two South American thugs was not on the agenda.'

'Poor Rafa,' said Maria. 'You certainly have been through the mill. However, I think there's a light at the end of this particular tunnel, Rafa and I'm sure you'll be alive to enjoy it. Felix, can you and Sandro go down to the bus stop and bring Chano back here. I'd like you, Rafa, to collect some items for me, then come back here and relax, while I make some sandwiches. We are all going to have a very busy and demanding afternoon and we'll need lots of stamina.'

'No problem, Maria. By the way, Rafa, where is Pedro today?'

'That's one question I do know the answer to. He will be in Tenerife all day. I don't know what he's doing and I don't want to know. He was taken in the minibus first thing this morning to San Sebastian and he is catching the last ferry back. The minibus is in use this morning collecting conference delegates from the airport so he couldn't borrow it all day. The minibus driver has to collect him from the ferry tonight and drop him off back home. It's a very long shift for him, but Pedro wouldn't consider that.'

'Not to worry, Rafa! At least you have a whole day without Pedro! That must be a massive bonus! I don't know how anyone works with Pedro. I certainly couldn't!'

Felix and Sandro hurried off to town to meet Chano. Maria outlined her plan to Rafa. He hugged her gratefully and went off happily to fetch the various items of equipment they might need. He felt huge relief, as if an enormous lead weight had been lifted off his head. There did appear to be some light at the end of the tunnel, though there were still many problems ahead. He hoped that their mission today would be successful and some good would come out of the evil. Then they would have to decide what to do about the next boatload of Africans, who were due the following night. Thank Heavens he had gone to Maria and Felix. They were the best friends in the world and he was such a lucky man. They had always treated him as part of their family and had been even more kind and caring after his wife had died. He hoped that one day he would be in a position to repay their kindness and compassion.

'I'm absolutely starving, Satya. My brain cells have been working overtime. Do you think the Professor would mind if we have an early lunch?'

'Probably not, in his present state of bonhomie! We won't ask. We'll just go to lunch though I think that today it might be sensible if we go separately, so that we can keep a beady eye on his whereabouts.'

'Good thinking, though it won't be nearly so pleasant without you munching quietly beside me and making fun of me. I won't be long. I promise.'

By the time everyone had returned, Maria had finished making a huge pile of sandwiches and more coffee. Introductions were made and coffee mugs passed round. The sitting-room positively buzzed with anticipation. Felix introduced Chano and invited him to regale them with his strange adventure on holiday which he had mentioned in his phone-call. Chano happily obliged and soon they were all laughing about the two unfit pilots wandering round Garajonay forest and then puffing up and down the precipitous ravines.

Suddenly Sandro stopped laughing and exclaimed:

'That's it. 'C' on the code means 'Chano' and 'D' stands for your co-pilot 'Domingo'. Let me show you the code, Chano. Perhaps it will mean more to you than it does to us.'

Sandro bounced over to the desk and retrieved the relevant piece of paper and notepad.

Chano studied it carefully for several minutes before he spoke.

'Well, perhaps I can help. 'TFN' probably stands for 'Tenerife North Airport' which is Los Rodeos. That's where the charter plane for the Centre here is mainly based, though we do collect and deliver delegates quite often to and from Reina Sofia Airport in the South, so I'm guessing that 'CP' stands for 'charter plane.' 'PDS' is probably 'Playa de Santiago Airport' here on La Gomera. I can check the dates against our time-sheets, if you want.'

'You're brilliant, Chano. I knew you would be able to unscramble the coded email. Would you have any idea what the rest of it means?' Maria was almost afraid to ask.

'I have a few shrewd ideas but let me finish telling you about what happened to us on holiday, while my brain is working subconsciously on your code.'

To a stunned audience, Chano related what had befallen them at the cave near the derelict factory. Then he explained how they had dutifully reported everything to the police, who had simply laughed at them and dismissed them as drunken idiots.

'I didn't think the police would listen,' said Maria. 'Rafa was fairly certain that they wouldn't help him either. I know you were invited for lunch, Chano and I will give you a great lunch next time you come, but we have an emergency on our hands today. If you are all willing,

I have a plan, well two plans in fact, depending on what we find when we arrive at La Rajita. The expedition is not without possible problems and considerable risk, but I think it is the only way we can do it.'

'Don't be so mysterious, Mum, and just tell us what we have to do,' pleaded Sandro.

'Certainly! But first let's demolish these sandwiches. We may be away some time.'

※

'I wonder what's happening back home,' said Ana. 'Dad told me that Mum was up half the night formulating some plan but I don't know exactly what she is going to do. Mum's brilliant at organisation.'

'I know she is,' replied Satya. 'I wish she were running this Conference Centre. It would make such a difference to everyone. I'm feeling rather drowsy this morning and can't concentrate properly. I feel a distinct requirement for a large black coffee. Shall I make you one, Ana?'

'No! No! I'll make you one, Satya. I'm not really concentrating at the moment either and need to do something simple like making coffee. I'm sorry there isn't any of Mum's cake, but I think there are a few cookies. I'll go and rustle up some refreshments.'

'Fantastic! Thanks, Ana. That would be much appreciated. It might just spur my brain cells into action.'

They reached the track which led down to La Rajita. They had waited patiently in Rafa's truck well hidden amongst the trees and shrubs until they hoped that the men from the factory had gone off towards Chipude, as they did every day at noon, regular as clockwork, according to Amit and Jeevan's report. At least Maria hoped fervently that the men had not deviated from their usual routine or they would have to abort their rescue mission. It would be foolhardy to continue where guns were involved.

'Sandro, I'd like you to stay here at the top of the track. Stay well hidden at all times. When the men return, whistle urgently to us. You can still remember the whistle language you learned at school, can't you?' Maria asked rather anxiously.

'Yes, I can, Mum. I was teaching some to Martin the other day, as it happens. I never thought I would ever use it again. Why don't you just ring me or text on the mobile?'

'Because we probably won't have a signal on the mobile down by the shore, so we'll have to whistle to each other. Okay, here's some drink and some cake while you wait. I know we have to take care of your stomach! Don't approach the men under any circumstances and don't come down the track unless we specifically ask you to. We'll pick you up as soon as we've finished. Dad or I will whistle to let you know what's happening.

If we don't whistle half an hour after the men have gone back down to the fish factory, then ring the police and tell them it is urgent, very urgent and they must come immediately. Thanks, Sandro, and don't worry. What you are going to do is very important. Just lie low and be patient. It may take quite a while. Just stay hidden at all times and keep safe!'

Rafa drove cautiously down the bumpy track and parked well out of sight behind the fish factory. There was no sign of the white van. He jumped out of the truck and fetched the items Maria had asked him to bring. Maria nervously kept watch while Felix and Chano climbed out of the back of the truck and helped Rafa. The windows of the factory were too high for them to see anything, so they had to go in blind. Maria hoped that she had calculated correctly that no-one else would be there except Karthik, the surgeon. She had briefed them all carefully on what they might have to do and she hoped they were not too late to rescue the surgeon. She prayed that no-one would get hurt. She was banking on the fact that the men would not have taken their weapons with them when they went off to lunch, as it would be too risky to carry the guns in the van in case the police stopped them for any reason.

With the bolt croppers Rafa soon undid the padlock on the metal doors of the factory and the three men armed with baseball bats warily entered the building, wondering fearfully what sights might greet them. They signalled to Maria that it was all going according to plan. She whistled 'all well' to Sandro and visibly relaxed when he whistled back.

Sara greeted her husband warmly as he arrived home from work. As he was on day shift this week, they could enjoy life more as a family. She hated the lonely nights when he was on duty at the Hotel. She could hardly wait to tell him some local news.

'Juan, you know that slimy two-faced solicitor, Diego Mendosa, on the High Street? He was arrested this morning by two uniformed policemen on charges of fraud and tax evasion. It caused quite a stir. No-one has ever liked him much; he was way too big-headed, but it's nevertheless a bit of a shock to find out he's a real criminal and has been fiddling the books and using clients' money from property deals for his own ends. He's been living the high life here for years exploiting the Canary Islanders. Apparently he's still got lots of property back in Spain as well.'

'I expect he'll find life very different in a prison in Spain. A bit of low life for him! I hope they lock up the miserable swine and let him rot. It's about time the corruption on these Islands was sorted out. They could start with the police. A lot of locals have not been prosecuted when they should, so no doubt there's a bribery scandal there waiting to be uncovered. It's not fair on the rest of us, who do obey the law.'

'That was the other bit of news I wanted to tell you, Juan. There's a new Chief Inspector come over from Barcelona and he's not best pleased with the local police force, apparently. He thinks they are bone idle and inefficient. The postman said there has been a lot of trouble down at the police station this week. His wife works there, you know, and she's been telling him all about it.'

'And half of the Islanders too, I've no doubt! Well, Sara, now that you have told me all the rumours that are flying around, do you think we could have some dinner? I'm absolutely starving. It's been a very long hot day.'

A man's body was lying inert in a steel cage, his wrists padlocked to the bars. Rafa set to work immediately with the bolt-croppers and snapped the padlock off the cage door. So far, so good. Felix and Chano went into the cage and lifted up the man's head and shoulders. They wanted to take some of the pressure off his wrists, so that Rafa could break open that padlock as well. The body was limp and unresponsive. Were they too late? Was he already dead? The man looked very poorly indeed.

'There's still a weak pulse,' said Chano, who as a charter pilot had to have basic medical training. 'I expect he's very dehydrated. Half-starved too, by the look of him. Poor devil! He must have been to hell and back in this place. How's it going, Rafa?'

Rafa looked up briefly and nodded. He carried on working steadily at the padlock. His stomach was churning with fear and disgust. He was trembling with the horror of what was all around them. They must succeed! They must stop this evil crime! This poor man must live! This wasn't sex trafficking! This was horror on a massive scale!

After what seemed hours, there was a metallic clunk and the man was free. Chano and Felix carried him carefully out to the truck and laid him on the blankets that Maria had brought in the hope of a successful outcome. She was relieved to see them, having been very worried that the rescue operation was taking so long. She gently put two pillows under the man's head. Then she indicated to Rafa, Felix and Chano to go and finish off inside the factory. Felix whistled to Sandro and was pleased to receive a reply. This operation was stretching their nerves to the limit and they were still only half-way through.

Maria talked quietly to the Indian in her care. She put one of the blankets over his wasted body. Warmth sometimes revived the spirit as well as the flesh. He was extremely weak, but at least he was still alive. The minutes ticked by agonisingly slowly. The man remained ominously still. She kept saying his name, 'Karthik' and squeezing his hand. Eventually the man stirred slightly and opened his eyes. He squinted in the sudden glare of bright sunshine which was piercing his subconscious. Maria carried on talking to him, reassuring him gently that he was safe now and repeating his name. She gave him a little water, cradling his head in her arms. His lips were so dry and cracked that most of the water just dribbled down his chin.

She could feel him relax a little as he slowly realised that he was out of the metal cage and out of the dreadful building. He could not believe it. Where were his two ghastly gaolers? Was he just hallucinating or was this for real? Was he really free at last? Who was this kind lady? Had he died and was on the other side with an angel ministering to him? This was truly a miracle. Someone had answered his prayers at last. Maria offered him some more water and he smiled gratefully at this miracle woman. He had thought he would never breathe fresh air again. He had accepted that death in the metal cage was inevitable and he would never see his family again, never see his homeland again, never fulfil his dreams. He had been totally resigned to his awful fate. He had no energy to resist any more. He was dead inside and assumed he would soon be dead outside as well. That lucrative eighteen-month research contract in Tenerife had seemed such a good idea.

Contracts were always fine on paper. Stark reality had proved horrendously different.

Rafa, Chano and her beloved Felix returned to the truck, relief written all over their faces. As Maria had predicted and desperately hoped, the guns had very obligingly been left in the factory and could shortly be put to good use. The element of surprise would be theirs. Now it was just a waiting game.

Karthik had taken some more water. A little colour was coming back into his face. They all touched his hand warmly and grinned. He was safe! It was incredible! He was going to live! It would take a long time for him to recover from the traumatic and dreadful conditions in which he had lived and worked, but live he would!

Suddenly they heard Sandro whistle urgently. Felix replied quickly. They all reacted instantly. Maria and Karthik lay down out of sight in the back of the truck. Rafa, Felix and Chano took up their positions, as planned. Everyone waited . . . . and waited . . . . and waited.

⁓≳⁓

Amit and Jeevan approached the forest hut very carefully and listened intently before throwing open the door. Nothing. No-one. The hut was still being used but there was no sign of the occupants. There were two apple cores and two peach stones on the desk and some crumbs, but otherwise the place was tidy and clean. They shrugged their shoulders, left the hut as they had found it and retreated into the forest to carry on their research work on the lichens. They would try again later. Sooner or later they would catch up with the illegal occupants of the forest hut. The 'squatters' weren't causing any damage. Jeevan had informed Satya who was not unduly worried and suggested that they keep a low profile and just check the hut periodically.

At last the white van wobbled into sight and came to a standstill where the track met the sand. The two men staggered out. They had obviously been drinking heavily. That would make them potentially violent and more difficult to deal with, but on the plus side, their brains would also be somewhat addled and that might be an advantage. They wandered unsteadily over the sand to the derelict building. While they were trying very awkwardly to find a key for the padlock, Felix and Chano stepped out from behind the factory, each pointing a shotgun at their victims. Rafa materialized out of nowhere and ordered them both to lie down on the ground spreadeagled. The two drunks didn't hesitate. Even in their alcoholic stupor they could recognise that the odds were stacked rather too heavily against them. Very quickly Rafa tied their wrists tightly behind their backs and then tied their ankles together even more tightly with the rope and heavy duty fishing line he had brought with him. One of the men attempted to kick him viciously, but Rafa quickly retaliated by rearranging the prisoner's private parts very deftly and the man crumpled up in pain and wisely decided that co-operation might be in his own best interests, if he ever wanted to father children. Felix wondered where Rafa had learned that interesting trick. He was certainly proving to be a great asset in these highly peculiar circumstances! Association with Pedro had obviously taught Rafa a great deal.

Rafa hauled the first prisoner unceremoniously up the steps into the old factory and then dragged him across the hard floor into the cage where they had found the poor Indian surgeon. He padlocked him to the cage, bolted the door behind him and went back to fetch his partner in crime. Chano stood guard over them, while Felix whistled the good news to Sandro and received confirmation that his son was in fine form. With the two men safely tied up and padlocked to the bars at opposite ends of the cage for double security, Rafa slammed the door to the cage shut and padlocked that as well. He was totally amazed how meticulously Maria had planned this operation. He would never have thought of half the details she had considered, such as new padlocks to replace the ones they would have cut open. She had also insisted that the prisoners should be padlocked in a sitting position, so they could not suffocate in their own vomit if they were very drunk. Felix had carefully confiscated the mobile phones, wallets, guns and keys for evidence for the police. Chano had taken copious photos on his mobile phone to prepare the authorities for what they would find. Such horror! Such a scene of atrocities! Such barbarism in the 21st century. They all hoped they would never see the like again. It was unbelievably horrendous!

The tension was easing now and Rafa had to admit that he was rather enjoying this bit of the rescue mission. Revenge for all those poor Africans! Revenge for the dreadful treatment of that poor surgeon. Poetic justice that the prisoners should for a while at least endure the degradation and suffering which they had inflicted so callously on others. The two thugs had pleaded, cajoled and tried to bribe their way out of their predicament, but Rafa had found two blood soaked rags and stuffed them rather roughly into their mouths. They were scum, vermin in his opinion and he wasn't going to waste time listening to them whining and whinging. They deserved to be tortured at the very least and left to die in a dark hole after the crimes which they had perpetrated.

Rafa, Felix and Chano walked back together to the truck and relayed the success of the operation to Maria. They were delighted to see Karthik looking a little more alert. Felix whistled to Sandro that they were on their way and Rafa and Chano climbed into the front of the truck with the tools Rafa had provided on Maria's instructions and all the confiscated property. Felix moved the van out of the way on to the beach, locked it and took the keys with him. He climbed into the back of the truck beside Maria. Rafa drove carefully up to the main road, where Sandro was waiting for them. He hopped quickly into the back of the truck. He was tense with excitement and Felix relayed some of the details of the rescue mission, as they made their uncomfortable way back home for a well-earned rest. Later they would inform the police, who could go and arrest the two culprits in the factory. Meanwhile the priority was to take Karthik home to the cottage to convalesce and recover from his ordeal, if that were possible. The authorities would not understand the extent of the terrible trauma he had endured and would not realise that he was in no state to cope with an interrogation for several days. Police intervention could wait until tomorrow, Maria decided.

※

'Relax, Ana! It will be all right. Maria will have planned everything very carefully and won't take any risks, I'm sure.'

'I know you're right, Satya, but I just wish one of them would text a progress report!'

Exactly on cue her mobile pinged and a text from her brother informed her that all had gone remarkably well. They had managed to rescue the Indian surgeon, who was very weak and suffering from dehydration and exhaustion. Hopefully, he would make a full recovery given time and lots of tender loving care. He also warned Ana to delete his text immediately for security reasons. Ana was so relieved by this news that she could hardly wait to go home. Satya decided it might be a good idea to distract her, as there was still another half hour before she could officially leave work and he did not want her worrying about the medical condition of the surgeon. However, before he could think of a topic to divert her attention, Ana suddenly asked him to tell her about India and the region where he grew up.

Satya was delighted and started to talk about the colour and vibrancy of India, the dust, the noise, the confusion of the cities and above all the warm hospitality—a land of stark contrasts. He soon realised, however, that Ana wasn't listening. He could have mentioned pink elephants and water melons the size of skyscrapers and she would have paid no attention. Her thoughts were elsewhere this afternoon and he would have to tell her about his homeland some other day when she could concentrate.

The adrenaline rush had subsided and exhaustion was setting in now. They were still elated by their success and had congratulated Maria several times on her brilliant organisation and extraordinarily meticulous planning. Eventually Rafa drew up outside the cottage. Sandro hopped agilely out of the truck, opened the front door wide and went through to the kitchen as instructed to make coffee for everyone. Felix, Rafa and Chano carried Karthik gently into the sitting-room and laid him down very carefully on the old leather sofa. Maria followed closely behind with the pillows and blankets and made the surgeon as comfortable as she could. Rafa and Chano went back out to the truck and brought in all the items they had confiscated from the two men at the fish factory and put them out of sight behind the sofa. Felix fetched extra chairs from the kitchen and Sandro brought in mugs of steaming coffee and a home-made sponge cake. He was starving, even if nobody else was! Rafa locked up the truck and went back into the cottage, closing the front door behind him. He fervently wished that he could shut out so easily the evil sights they had witnessed that afternoon.

Maria helped Karthik to drink some warm milk into which she had put a dash of brandy. He was obviously still in a severe state of shock. Since he was warm and safe now, she hoped that the brandy's restorative powers would help in this instance. He was so pale and weak, but he nevertheless tried very hard to speak. His voice was hoarse and raucous and the sound which emerged was incomprehensible. Yet they all realised that he was trying to thank them and they beamed back at him. There was a warm companionship in the room and the atmosphere was charged with many conflicting emotions.

'I can't believe I ignored what was going on,' said Rafa in despair. 'I can't believe I was so apathetic and so selfish that I did nothing to find out more about the racket and try to stop it. I thought it was perhaps a sort of modern slave trade. I never imagined it could be something so awful. How can I live with myself?'

Felix put his arm round his friend and tried to comfort him.

'You weren't in a position to do anything, Rafa. You would have lost your life if you had tried to intervene. You know Pedro only too well. No-one could have imagined what was going on at that factory. You were fantastic today. We couldn't have managed without your skill and knowledge. You have more than made up for any inaction before.'

'Don't blame yourself for anything at all, Rafa,' said Maria, endorsing her husband's sentiments. 'You were invaluable today. I did the theoretical planning based on a few hunches but without you none of this rescue mission would have been possible.'

'I'm glad my brute force and ignorance were useful for once,' smiled Rafa.

'Your driving wasn't bad either, Rafa!' Sandro said jokingly.

'We were a great team! Thank you everyone for each and every contribution. We did incredibly well. I feel a little guilty about the two prisoners we left in the factory, but a taste of their own medicine might make them realise what they have done to innocent men. I hope they enjoy their night in a cold damp cage!'

'I wish we could leave them to rot there. They deserve it. I have never encountered two such callous individuals.' Chano shuddered as he recalled the nightmarish scene.

'Would you like to come with us to the police station tomorrow, Chano?'

'Yes, I would, if I may. I'd like to see this through and I shall have great pleasure seeing the faces of the policemen when they realise I was telling them the truth and they did nothing about it. It's my day off tomorrow but I can come across with Domingo in the morning. The plane will have plenty of empty seats. We land at 1030 hrs.'

'I'll pick you up at the airport, if you like,' volunteered Rafa. 'I'm not working until tomorrow night.'

Suddenly Rafa put his head in his hands and almost wailed in despair.

'Maria, what can we do about the Africans coming tomorrow? I'd completely forgotten about them with all the events of this afternoon.'

'We'll talk to the police tomorrow morning. With all the evidence we have, they can't ignore this racket. They will have to act. We'll find some way to keep you safe, Rafa. Pedro won't be able to hurt you. He will soon be out of your life for ever.'

'I hope you're right, Maria. I don't know what I would have done without your intervention. I can't thank you enough for helping me in this dire situation.'

'You're worth helping, Rafa,' said Felix and Maria almost simultaneously.

Maria gave Karthik some more milk and asked Sandro to heat up a little of the rice pudding currently residing on the top shelf of the fridge.

'I don't know if this is the right time to tell you, but I've worked out the rest of the code, in theory at least. How it works in practice I'm not too sure at this stage.'

'Well done, Chano! That's very clever of you. Please do explain it all!'

'It's not clever really. It's just that the code relates so closely to what Domingo and I are doing, so it's obvious to us but would not be apparent to any of you.'

Just then Sandro came back with a small dish of rice pudding for the surgeon. With Maria's help he managed to eat about half of it and then lay back on the pillows, exhausted. Maria motioned to him to sleep and smiled at him encouragingly. Gratefully, he closed his eyes and drifted off into peaceful oblivion. A good night's sleep in a safe environment was the best treatment he could have wished for.

'What time do you need to be back at the airport, Chano?' asked Felix anxiously. 'Have you time for supper? I promise we'll feed you much better next time you come!'

'I ought to head off shortly,' replied Chano. 'I always like to be there in plenty of time in case there is a lot of cargo to load up first. You have fed me very well, actually!'

'Rafa, would you like to drop Chano off at the airport and then come back here for supper? I'll go and buy some pizzas or similar. Maria is very tired and I don't want her cooking tonight. How does that sound?' asked Felix.

'Wonderful,' replied Rafa 'but you stay here with the family and I'll pick up something edible on the way back from the airport. And, no, I don't want any money, thank you. Buying you all supper is the least I can do!'

Chano hugged Maria and Felix and followed Rafa out to the truck. He felt drained and would be glad when the flight to Tenerife was over and he could settle down quietly at home and reflect on the events of the day. He would update Domingo in the morning.

Just under thirty minutes later Rafa arrived back at the cottage with various packages of hot food in brightly coloured carrier bags.

'That smells good, Rafa! You've certainly brought plenty! Thank you very much indeed. I must say I feel quite exhausted now and have no inclination whatever to cook after such an eventful day. It's very thoughtful of you. Feel free to come anytime!'

'It was Felix's idea,' replied Rafa, smiling at Maria. 'He assumed that you would be very tired after you were up half the night planning the rescue mission. I think you're just amazing. I don't know how you worked it all out. It all went like clockwork.'

'There was an awful lot of guesswork involved,' said Maria. 'I'm just relieved that we managed to achieve what we set out to do. I planned several scenarios and possible outcomes and some weren't very pleasant, but luck was on our side, thank goodness, and all went well.'

'I hope you haven't ruined that chap's matrimonial prospects!' interjected Felix. 'Was that strategic move part of the ordained plan? You reacted very quickly to the situation. I was seriously impressed!'

They were all laughing when Ana arrived home. She assumed that it was Karthik fast asleep on the sofa and was eager to hear the details of what had transpired during the day.

'Let's tuck in to this delicious food before it goes cold,' suggested Maria. 'We've really earned our supper tonight. We'll tell you all about it, Ana, while we demolish this interesting array of take-aways, which

Rafa has very kindly bought for us and your Dad has laid out on the table.'

'Wow! Rafa! What a feast! You must definitely come more often!'

'Sandro, please don't tease Rafa! He's had a very hard day,' admonished Felix.

In between mouthfuls, Felix and Rafa described the rescue mission to Ana, being very careful to omit details of what they had found in the factory itself. They suspected that Maria had already worked out what the building was being used for, but there was no need to burden Ana or Sandro with that information at this stage.

'Mum, you're amazing! How on earth did you manage to plan all that?'

'Planning was the easy part, Ana! It was the execution that could have been difficult to perhaps impossible. Fortunately, thanks to our intrepid 'musketeers' it was a great success and your Indian surgeon is alive, even if he is far from well. It is going to take Karthik a long time to recover from such a traumatic experience, but he is welcome to stay for as long as it takes. Meanwhile, no-one, absolutely no-one must know that he is here until everyone involved in this criminal activity has been arrested and taken into custody. Tomorrow, Ana, you and Satya must act normally and say nothing until the Professor has been arrested. If he suspects anything at all, he will disappear and re-emerge somewhere else in the world and commit this awful crime again. We must not allow that to happen.'

'He told us this afternoon that he would be in the office again tomorrow, as he is still catching up on paperwork,' said Ana. 'I'll text you immediately if he goes out.'

'Rafa, you're welcome to stay the night here, if you don't mind a camp bed in Sandro's room. I don't think he snores, so you might get a reasonable night's sleep!'

'Thanks, Felix, but it might be best not to leave the truck parked outside your cottage. It might alert Pedro that something is going on. He has spies everywhere, you know. He frightens people into giving him information they didn't even know they knew. He's a very shrewd cookie and it's best to play safe. I'll go back home now and have a shower and get some kip, hopefully. Then I'll pick Chano up from the airport tomorrow morning and come down here to collect Maria. Then we'll head off to the police station where we shall have the dubious pleasure of telling them about the Professor's criminal organisation.'

'That would be great, Rafa. Felix, I know you want to come too, but I think it would be a good idea if you and Sandro stayed here quietly and looked after Karthik. He will probably be very anxious and upset tomorrow and may require two of you to keep him calm and stress-free. Hopefully, this will all be over by tomorrow evening and we can invite Satya down to talk to him. He will relax more if he is talking in his native tongue. I don't know how much English or Spanish he knows, but it would put more strain on him to express himself in a foreign language and we want him to relax and recover gently. Poor man, it's a long hard road ahead for him!'

'That makes sense, Maria. Sandro and I will take good care of Karthik in your absence, won't we, Sandro?'

'No worries, Mum. Is there plenty of food in the fridge?'

'You and your stomach, Sandro! You must have worms! I don't know where you put all this food! I don't think you'll starve tomorrow, if that's what you're thinking!' said Maria, laughing despite her tiredness.

'I'll be off, then,' said Rafa. 'Thank you all for everything. I'll see you in the morning.'

'Thanks again for all your help, Rafa,' said Felix, embracing his friend warmly.

'Thanks for the supper, Rafa. Please, please come again!' pleaded Sandro grinning.

Rafa gave everyone a brief hug. Maria went with him to the front door and whispered to him to sleep well and not to worry. He nodded briefly, looking considerably happier than he had that morning. He hugged her again, gratefully. He climbed into the battered old truck, which had provided such valiant service that day and headed somewhat anxiously for his empty home.

'Go on up to bed, all of you and get some sleep! I'll stay down here with Karthik. He will probably be confused when he wakes up and I don't want him to panic. Also he needs lots of drink and he may even feel like some food,' said Felix.

'He is very dehydrated and probably ought to be on a saline drip, but he is more alert now than when we found him,' said Maria, 'so I think he will be all right. He is safe here and I don't think he would cope with the long trip to the hospital at the moment. The journey here from La Rajita was bad enough for him. It's probably better that he rests quietly and relaxes here. In the circumstances a hospital is probably the last place on earth that he would want to be! A homely family environment is just what he needs at the moment. I know we are all strangers to him, but he knows we have his best interests at heart and he feels secure and protected here.'

'You're right, Mum, as always. I suppose I had better wait until tomorrow night until I email Tamarai to let her know that her father is safe.'

'Yes, Ana, please wait. One more day won't make that much difference. We can't afford to jeopardise this operation in any way. As soon as all the criminals are under lock and key, you can tell her the good news. Come on, everyone! Time for bed!'

Once the twelve passengers had disembarked, Chano emerged from the co-pilot seat, bade Domingo a cheery farewell and crossed the tarmac to where Rafa was waiting in the familiar old truck. He greeted Rafa warmly and climbed in quickly beside him.

'Did you manage to get any sleep last night, Rafa?' Chano enquired of his new friend.

'Best night's sleep I've had for weeks!' replied Rafa. 'I'm so glad I went to Felix and Maria with all my worries. They are the best friends you could wish for and I hope that I can repay their kindness one day. I know I shall probably be prosecuted as an accessory to the crime, even though I didn't know what the crime was! Maria thinks that I may escape with a caution as I helped with the operation to free the Indian surgeon. I think I deserve to pay for my apathetic attitude. At least now I have a clear conscience which is why I actually managed to sleep. I thought I would have nightmares, but everything was okay until I woke up this morning and then I remembered the Africans coming tonight. I'm really scared and panicking, but if anyone can sort it out, it is Maria. I trust her judgment completely and shall do whatever she suggests.'

'She's an amazing lady!' agreed Chano. 'I'm so pleased I started up a conversation with you and Felix down by the harbour that morning. I feel privileged to have met you all, even though the whole situation is somewhat bizarre! Such an unusual set of coincidences to help us solve such a heinous crime! The Professor will be shocked that his secret has been uncovered by a bunch of amateurs! He must have made a fortune out of this racket. The Indian government will be furious that he has tried to bring the Centre into disrepute. Maria is hoping that the scandal can be handled in such a way that the Centre remains open and the locals keep their jobs, as unemployment here is so high.'

When they reached the cottage, they saw Maria waiting quietly in the porch with a folder of documents in her hand. Chano hopped out of the truck and went over to her. They embraced warmly. Maria asked him to take a photo of Karthik to show to the police and collect the confiscated property from behind the leather sofa. Chano willingly obliged. Then they both went out to the truck together, carrying the incriminating evidence.

'You can have a front seat today, Maria! No extra charge! You'll find it vastly more comfortable than in the back of this decrepit old truck!'

'Thank you, Rafa. I must say I didn't fancy being bruised and bumped all the way to San Sebastian. There's not much suspension on this vehicle of yours!'

'Okay, Rafa,' said Chano. 'Let's go and get this over with. It will be interesting to see what sort of reception we are given.'

Felix had slept fitfully in the old armchair. At intervals during the night he had persuaded Karthik to drink some more water and eat a little more of the rice pudding. Maria had made scrambled eggs for them both for breakfast with toast for Felix. She didn't want to risk Karthik choking on toast until he had taken more liquid. He gratefully accepted some more warm milk with honey. She was relieved that Karthik felt relaxed in the cottage. Progress would be slow, but at least he was now more in the land of the living than he had been twenty-four hours previously.

Another twenty-four hours and it would have been too late. He was painfully thin and had obviously lost the will to live and felt that death was the only way out of the ghastly scenario at the factory. Maria gave instructions to Felix for Karthik's welfare and promised she would ring with any news as soon as they had left the police station.

Despite roadworks and a broken down car partially obstructing the highway, they reached the capital, San Sebastian, in good time. Surprisingly, Rafa managed to park right opposite the police station. Apprehensively, he and Chano walked into the modern building behind a very purposeful Maria, who was clearly ready to do battle with the authorities. She dealt with the civilian receptionist very efficiently and after a short wait they were ushered into the august presence of the new Chief Inspector from Barcelona.

Meanwhile Sandro had packed his father off to bed to 'catch up on his beauty sleep,' as he cheekily put it. He promised he would call him immediately if he needed help with their patient, Karthik. Playfully cuffing his son, Felix went upstairs to rest. He seriously doubted that he would fall asleep, as he was nervous about what might be happening to Maria, Rafa and Chano. He hoped and prayed that Rafa would not be arrested.

Maria quietly introduced everyone to the Inspector, who courteously invited them to sit down. They all perched rather nervously on the uncomfortable chairs in his office. Then without any preamble Maria launched into her account and zoomed straight to the main points. As soon as she mentioned the word 'murder' the Inspector's attention was riveted on the three visitors in his office. Maria explained how the Professor of the new Indian Conference Centre had masterminded the crime. She handed him a printout of the Professor's mobile calls and contacts, which Sandro had done for her. She suggested that they should investigate the Professor's bank accounts as soon as possible and stop any large or unusual transactions leaving the country.

'Delegates arrived from all over the world to attend the various conferences at the Centre on 'Alternative Energy Sources' and 'Conservation' but that was just a front to hide the Professor's real activities. Some of the Indian delegates went to the Conference Centre, then back to the new clinic near the airport in Tenerife, where they received organ transplants. All sorts of operations were performed, from simple corneal transplants to very complex multiple transplants such as heart and lung, liver and pancreas, kidneys and pancreas etc. As there is an acute shortage of donated organs available in India, these rich 'delegates' were prepared to pay incredible amounts to have whatever they needed to prolong their lives,' explained Maria. 'Unfortunately,' continued Maria, 'some of the operations went disastrously wrong and the patients died.'

The Inspector was sitting bolt upright listening to her in horror and trepidation.

'How on earth did you work all this out?' He asked in admiration.

'An interesting series of coincidences,' replied Maria, 'and the generous and unstinting help of my friends here.'

Maria then asked Chano to show the Inspector the photos he had taken at the fish factory.

The silence in the office was palpable, as the policeman stared at the photos on Chano's mobile phone. Any shred of doubt he might have harboured while listening to Maria's account had vanished. He was obviously extremely distressed by what he was viewing.

Maria continued the incredible tale. She described how Indian surgeons had been unwittingly recruited to remove the organs from the unwilling victims in the first place and then to transplant them into the rich recipients in the Clinic in Tenerife. At least one of the surgeons at the Clinic had refused to continue with the operations because the donor organs were not compatible with the recipients. He found the situation completely unethical because he knew that the transplant organs would be rejected and the recipients would die, despite all the anti-rejection drugs, the so-called immuno-suppressants, which they would be given at the Clinic.

'Obviously,' she continued, 'this surgeon was asking too many questions and becoming an embarrassment to them. They couldn't let him fly back to India, because he knew too much. In fact, he had sort of signed his own death warrant. So he disappeared mysteriously just over three weeks ago. They effectively took him prisoner, ferried him across here to La Gomera and made him work at the old fish factory at La Rajita at gunpoint. My daughter, Ana, accidentally came across several frantic emails from his daughter in India, asking for help in locating him. My son tracked him down to the Clinic and he was alive and well about three weeks ago. Then I overheard the Professor talking on the phone one day about 'Karthik', which I incorrectly assumed was a place, not a person. Then Chano came to lunch yesterday with new information and we collated all the evidence and decided to go to the old fish factory and try to rescue the surgeon. Depending on what we found there, we would either abort the mission or continue. My assumptions were fortunately correct and the rescue was successful.'

At this juncture Maria handed over to Chano to relate the details of what he had discovered on his walking holiday with Domingo. He explained to the Inspector that he and his friend were the pilots of the plane chartered by the Indian Conference Centre. As such, they transferred delegates all over the archipelago as required. After a very hectic schedule they had taken a few days off. They decided to spend the time on La Gomera and on the third day of their holiday had found their way to a cave near the beach at La Rajita. He relayed the strange sequence of events there to the Inspector and concluded by saying that they had dutifully reported all the strange goings-on to the police in this very station and had been ridiculed and humiliated by the staff on duty.

'We realised then that we would have to try to rescue the Indian surgeon ourselves as the police assumed that we were raving lunatics and had made the whole thing up. This amazing lady here planned the whole operation and we succeeded in rescuing the surgeon, Karthik Nayar, yesterday afternoon,' finished Chano, rather breathlessly.

'Where is he now?' asked the Inspector, still trying to come to terms with the horror.

'Maria is taking really good care of him at her home. Well, her son and husband are doing it today while we are here. He is very frail and totally exhausted. He has been starved and badly beaten. He can't even speak yet but he knows he is safe now and will see his family and homeland again one day,' said Rafa.

'He's in the best possible place,' added Chano. 'If anyone can get him better, then that person is Maria. He is very traumatised by his ordeal, as you can imagine, but her tender loving care will be the best medicine he could ever have.'

When Felix came downstairs two hours later after a refreshing sleep, he could hear that the patient was snoring gently. Sandro was sitting quietly beside him, doing a crossword.

'He has hardly stirred,' said Sandro. 'I gave him some boiled rice water about an hour ago and he went off to sleep again. He must be absolutely exhausted, poor man.'

'He seems a gentle soul,' added Felix. 'I'm so glad we reached him in time.'

'I wonder how Mum, Rafa and Chano are faring at the police station. I hope we'll hear something soon.'

'I hope so, too,' responded his father. 'All this waiting around for news makes me extremely nervous.'

***

'You seem to have quite a fan club!' commented the Inspector, looking admiringly at the extremely attractive lady seated in front of him. 'Thank you for all you have done, even if your methods appear to have been highly unorthodox, to say the least!'

'I apologise for that,' said Maria smiling, 'but we knew we had to act quickly. This is where Rafa comes into the story. This is also where we need your help, your sympathy, your compassion and your understanding. Rafa has been blackmailed and coerced into helping his employer. He had no idea what he was involved in and could have done very little about it even if he had known the terrible truth. He accepts blame for what he unwittingly did, but without his invaluable help yesterday, we could not have achieved what we did.

He is a good kind man and would never willingly hurt anyone.'

Rafa smiled his heartfelt thanks at Maria and proceeded to tell the Inspector about the boatloads of Africans who were transported to La Rajita; how he had assumed it was sex-trafficking or a modern version of the slave trade; how he was terrified of Pedro, his employer; how he had eventually gone to Maria and her husband, Felix, for help and advice; how he had done his best yesterday to put things right; how guilty he felt for not doing something about the racket earlier.

Maria interrupted Rafa and looked straight into the Inspector's eyes.

'Rafa would have ended up dead, if he had tried to intervene in any way. I'm sure you will appreciate the impossible situation he was in, Sir. He was absolutely brilliant yesterday on our rescue mission. However, he is still in grave danger from his employer. There is another boatload of Africans coming across tonight. The rendezvous is at 2130 hours and Rafa will have to be there with Pedro to transfer them into the trawler and take them to La Rajita as usual. If Rafa doesn't turn up, then Pedro will smell a very unsavoury rodent. Pedro will escape the clutches of the law, the Africans will perish at sea in their leaky boat and Rafa will probably be murdered by Pedro for ruining his very lucrative trade. I have a suggestion which may work but it will need careful organisation and co-ordination. I don't think we want any more blood spilled!'

'Are you after my job, Maria?' asked the Inspector, grinning despite the serious situation.

'You seem to have the whole situation under control, while I am still trying to come to terms with the horror and the complexities of the case!'

'No! Definitely not! We have had much longer than you to evaluate the situation. Thank you for listening to our account and taking us seriously. May I outline a further plan of action to you and you can see whether it is feasible? We need to act quickly and efficiently, if you want to have all the culprits behind bars tonight.'

'All in good time! Can I just clarify a few points so that I know I am in full possession of the facts, before we go any further?' asked the Inspector. 'Number One: What happened to the Africans after they went to the old fish factory at La Rajita?'

'The organs which were required for transplant were surgically removed from these unfortunate Africans and put into storage ready for onward transfer to the Clinic in Tenerife,' explained Chano as unemotionally as he could manage. 'We think that the mutilated Africans were then killed and their bodies were burned in a big bonfire on the beach. We found evidence of that when we were down there yesterday. Those poor Africans met a very gruesome end. They had hoped to start a new life on the Islands and instead met a terrible death.'

The Inspector digested this unpalatable information and asked his second question.

'What happened to the two armed guards?'

'Yes, we were coming to that,' said Maria innocently. 'We had to make sure they didn't escape before we managed to inform the police, so we thought they wouldn't mind a dose of their own medicine. They are padlocked to the filthy cage inside the fish factory, where they had kept the Indian surgeon prisoner. We have the keys to the padlocks here, also their wallets for identification, their guns for confiscation and their mobile phones. We also have the keys to their van which is parked on the beach. There you will find the DNA of two Indian gentlemen, whose transplants were unsuccessful. I suspect they died in the factory and were subsequently incinerated.'

'Good Heavens! Are you telling me that you have left the two criminals locked up in a metal cage since yesterday afternoon?' queried the Inspector somewhat incredulously.

'It's really just the same as a cell,' replied Maria in a conciliatory fashion. 'We couldn't get a signal on any of our mobile phones, so we couldn't alert you. We had to improvise and make sure the two thugs could not escape. We also couldn't be certain at that point that the police would believe us and we wanted you to catch all the criminals involved in this evil crime, not just a few of the henchmen.'

The Inspector stared at the curious trio opposite him. He was for once speechless. He felt that he needed somehow to regain control of this bizarre situation for the honour of the police force. Since the said police force had however already ignored the crime correctly reported to them and insulted and alarmed these good people to such an extent that they had felt obliged to take the law into their own hands, he was at a complete loss to know how to continue. The three people opposite him seemed to have succeeded where conventional policing would probably have failed miserably. He now had every confidence that the plan which Maria had formulated for the evening's events would be more intelligent and more carefully evaluated than any he or his colleagues could devise at such short notice.

'Right,' he said more decisively than he felt. 'First of all, I'll order up some coffee for all of us. Personally, I could do with a stiff brandy after what you've told me, but I'll have one or two later when this peculiar day is over. While we're waiting, Maria, could you please outline your rescue plan to me. We'll also have to work out the best time to arrest the Professor and your captives at the fish factory at La Rajita. Time is of the essence, so we won't bother with any paperwork now. We'll take statements from you all later on. After seeing what you have achieved so far, I feel I can trust your assessment of the situation. Whilst I cannot condone your methods, I must concede that you all acted in good faith and I can only apologise for the appalling behaviour of the staff here. They failed miserably in their duty towards you, but I shall deal with that problem later when all the criminals are safely tucked up in the cells. Meanwhile, let's have some refreshments and organise the next stage of this operation!'

'Dad, what's taking them so long? The suspense is killing me! Have they arrested them for locking up those two gunmen? Have they not believed what they were saying? Have they arrested Rafa for transferring the Africans? Has Mum been arrested for planning it all? I'm getting really worried.'

'Don't worry, Sandro! Your mother knows exactly what she's doing. She has collected lots of evidence to back up her case. It's a very complex situation and it's going to take a considerable time to explain everything, especially as the police will probably be very sceptical. Then they have to plan a detailed operation for tonight for the refugees and also for Rafa's safety. It's bound to take a long time and it will seem even longer to us, because we are waiting so anxiously.'

'Mum will be pleased that Karthik is looking brighter. I'm glad you were there, Dad, when he woke up. He was very confused and panicky, as Mum predicted. How exactly does Mum manage to anticipate everyone's reactions so well?'

'Your Mum is one very clever lady, Sandro, and we are so lucky to have her.'

'You're absolutely right, Dad. We'd be lost without her. I suppose I inherited all my brains from Mum,' said Sandro teasingly.

'What brains, young man?' Felix playfully cuffed his ears, as they settled down happily together to wait.

⁂

Maria, Rafa and Chano were standing outside the police station, exhausted but relieved.

'Thank goodness that's over!' said Maria, with a heartfelt sigh. 'It went much better than I had expected. The Inspector was most co-operative, I think.'

'He was putty in your hands!' laughed Chano. 'I think he was scared stiff of you. He also realised that your master plan was excellent and he would be unlikely to come up with anything better at such short notice.'

'I can't believe I am still a free man. I can't thank you enough, Maria. You are a miracle worker. The Inspector is fairly confident that I will get off with a caution or a suspended sentence at worst, if any of it does come to court. Thank you so much, Maria.'

'That was a masterstroke of yours, Maria. If the situation is dealt with very discreetly, as you suggested to the Inspector, there won't be any bad publicity for the Islands and tourism won't be affected. If there's no publicity, then they may be able to persuade the Indian government to keep the Centre running and then all the locals at the Centre and the Conference Hotel will be able to keep their much needed jobs and Domingo and I will be able to keep our jobs as well. Yesterday I could see the spectre of unemployment staring me in the face, but today I feel more hopeful, thanks to you.'

'Let's hope it all goes according to schedule tonight. Are you okay with the plan, Rafa? I'm afraid I couldn't think of any other way of doing it.' Maria was clearly concerned.

'I'll be okay,' replied Rafa. 'My nightmare will be over soon, if all goes well tonight.'

'I've just sent a text to Sandro and Felix,' said Maria. 'Just to update them. I'm not going to text Ana or Satya. It will be better if they know nothing in advance. Let's get you back to the airport, Chano. Next week when you have some free time, we'll go out together and celebrate. This will all be behind us and we can relax and enjoy each other's company. Please bring Domingo too, if he would like to come. I'm sorry you have had to spend your day off at the police station, but we'll make it up to you!'

'It's been time well spent, Maria. Job done! I've also had the pleasure of your company and Rafa's and it's great to have made such lovely new friends.'

Rafa opened the door of the truck for Maria and Chano. One part of his ordeal was over. Now he had only to survive the evening sortie with his unpredictable employer, Pedro. He hoped that the police would adhere rigidly to Maria's subtle plan and not jeopardise his rather delicate situation by inventing a different strategy at the last minute.

It was late afternoon when three men entered the Professor's office. The Professor was completely nonplussed. Three men had just barged unannounced into his office! Three men had dared to violate his sanctuary! Rigid with tension and anger, the Professor stared uncomprehendingly at his unwelcome visitors, who had closed the door to his office and now stood menacingly in a row blocking his escape. He continued to glare at the spokesman who had begun to explain the reason for their sudden appearance in his personal space.

Gradually the Professor's expression changed from consummate fury to genuine alarm and then more rapidly to cold terror. This could not be happening. He had been so careful not to leave any evidence which could be traced back to himself. He was so sure he had obliterated his tracks. Nothing could possibly have connected him with the Clinic in Tenerife, could it? Any relevant emails had been encrypted in case anyone unauthorised accessed them. Phone calls were made on his mobile, not on the Centre's landline, so that they could not be traced. That hideous fisherman would never have talked. He had far too much to lose and nothing whatever to gain by spilling the beans. The other couriers knew nothing of any consequence. The contact in West Africa only had his mobile number and knew nothing else about him. He had deliberately never set foot in the new Clinic that Carlos had set up in Tenerife. They always met up on Lanzarote to spend time together. Their only contact was by mobile and he usually deleted any data. They had been so very careful. Carlos had all the underworld contacts necessary for the various scams. It was he who had recruited the two Venezuelan guards for the factory and the West African trader. It was he who had employed that devious solicitor on the Island but he had paid Mendosa very well for all his underhand dealings. Mendosa had recommended Pedro but knew nothing of the scam. Mendosa had sold Carlos the derelict factory but he could have had no idea what the building was used for. Mendosa had never been to the Conference Centre or the Clinic. Mendosa had never met either of them. Carlos had always dealt with him by phone. Therefore it could not have been the solicitor who had betrayed him. How on earth had anyone managed to work out any of this and in such incontrovertible detail? This was impossible. This could not be happening to him. Had they become complacent with their success? Had they tripped up somewhere? He must warn Carlos. He must talk to Carlos. But how? He turned abruptly and stared unseeingly out of the window. Where had they made a mistake? The world outside his office window looked completely normal and serene. What could possibly have gone wrong?

The voice droned on with the details of the crimes of which he stood accused. The Professor heard nothing. He had shrunk into himself, seemingly defeated. The small wiry figure stood immobile, impassive, apparently deaf to the accusations raining down on him. He tried to summon up a few shreds of dignity and turned to face his tormentors. He offered to accompany them to the police station to clarify various points and explain their misconceptions. There was obviously a misunderstanding and he would be more than happy to explain anything they wished, but he was of course innocent of any crime and did not appreciate defamation and slander of his character. The Professor seemed to be recovering his arrogant self-confidence and continued to protest his innocence. At a signal from the Inspector one of the men stepped forward, yanked the Professor's hands behind his back quite unceremoniously and handcuffed him. The Professor was clearly taken aback. This was outrageous. This was not really happening. This was a nightmare. He would wake up in a moment and normality would be restored. But it was happening and the reality of his situation was slowly dawning on him.

He could not bluster his way out of this. This was real. He had been arrested. He had been hand-cuffed in his own office. He would shortly be taken out of the safety of this Conference Centre which he had so carefully planned and developed into an unknown zone which was well beyond his control.

Shock and grim realization were slowly seeping into his very existence. He was about to lose everything. Why? How? Who had betrayed him? How much could the authorities prove? He had not personally done anything wrong. He was innocent, wasn't he? Of course he was! Surely no-one could know that he and Carlos were the brains behind the whole operation. He had never personally committed any crime. How could he be guilty of murder, as they claimed? His hands were clean. Others had done the dirty work. How did these policemen know all this? The plan had been foolproof. They had spent two years perfecting the organisation. What on earth had gone wrong? Apart from the large profits for himself and Carlos, he had of course been motivated by the desire to help his fellow countrymen. Did these three idiots not understand that? It was a complete misinterpretation of the facts. It would all be clarified and life would return to normal, wouldn't it? When would he see Carlos again? Had Carlos been arrested? Had anyone even mentioned his name? He hadn't been concentrating. How stupid! He had been in shock. The Professor, clearly agitated and annoyed, slumped down into his chair.

The Inspector's voice interrupted his frantic musings and demanded his immediate attention. The Professor meekly replied that his mobile was in his back pocket and one of the officers quickly and efficiently relieved him of it. The other officer undertook a rapid body search, which obviously upset the Professor's dignity. He did not, however, protest too much. He had already subsided into a defeated heap. The humiliation of it! These moronic officials would pay for this! How dare they treat him like this! He was a very important person. Did these fools not know that? He would not tolerate such treatment from local officialdom! Eventually the Professor stopped blustering and subsided miserably into a cold silence born of fury and frustration.

The Inspector duly informed the Professor that he was under arrest, but that he would remain at the Centre with these two officers until after dark because of the peculiar circumstances of the case. He would then be transferred to the police station at San Sebastian, where he would be able to help them with their enquiries with a solicitor present, if he so wished. He would have adequate opportunity at that point in time to give his explanation of the various events which had led to his arrest. They would meanwhile search the premises for any incriminating evidence, as a search warrant had already been granted for that purpose. The Inspector stopped talking and looked closely at the Professor, who was a crumpled picture of despair and abject misery. How could such an eminent academic have masterminded such an abominable crime? No punishment would ever fit that heinous crime. It rarely did, he reflected.

Satya was still sitting at his desk, wondering what was happening down the corridor. He had met the three plain clothes policemen at Reception as arranged earlier and had authorised their entry to the Centre as 'visiting associates' so as not to alert either Security or the Professor to their real identity. Everything was being kept as low key as possible to avert any scandal or rumours, which might jeopardise the potential future of the Centre. Ana had left for home some time ago, eager to see her mother and hear a detailed account of events. Satya would go over to Ana's later when he had discharged his duties at the Centre. He was looking forward to meeting Felix and Karthik. Meanwhile he had to wait for news from the Inspector. The Conference Hotel Manager had an appointment with the Professor in five minutes and he was in for a very unpleasant surprise. He, too, would be arrested and would be confined to the Professor's office, until word came through that Pedro and Rafa had left the harbour to rendezvous with the next boatload of Africans. At that point Satya had to take the policemen and their two 'prisoners' down to Reception. He would have to pretend he was talking normally to colleagues in order to let them all through Security without arousing any suspicion. He hoped that the Professor and the Hotel Manager could be 'persuaded' to go along with this strategy and thereby avoid any upsetting scenes in front of any members of staff who might still be in the building.

After driving Chano to the airport to catch his flight back to Los Rodeos, Rafa had dropped Maria off at home and continued down to the supermarket near the harbour. He parked the truck nearby and went in to stock up on biscuits and drinks for the refugees he would rescue that evening and some basic supplies for himself. He was trying hard to be calm and unhurried, but his mind and body were already in turmoil in anticipation of the forthcoming ordeal. By midnight he could either be dead or badly injured. He was much less certain of the outcome now that Maria was not by his side. At least the weather forecast was good for tonight, so the transfer should be relatively trouble-free. He hoped that Pedro would not have imbibed too much alcohol by the time they left the harbour. He didn't need the additional complication of a drunken employer. Whatever happened tonight, Rafa was glad he had confided in Maria and Felix. Their role in solving the crime was to remain confidential, so he had not endangered the lives of his best friends. What could he ever do to repay them?

Maria arrived home to a fantastic welcome from her husband and son. They were so relieved to see her and wanted to hear all about the proceedings at the police station. She was delighted to see Karthik sitting up in the armchair and smiling contentedly at her. Sandro made coffee for his parents and some hot lemon and honey for their guest. Karthik beckoned to Maria and she went across to him. He took her hands into his own and looked gratefully at her before saying quietly and hoarsely in rather stilted English:

'Thank you all so much. You saved my life. I had no hope. No escape for me. No way out. I felt so stupid. So stupid to accept that contract. I thought it was only research. I never imagined the operations. I had to do many terrible things.'

'No-one could have predicted that,' said Maria, trying to console Karthik. 'You were innocently caught up in an international crime of horrendous proportions. It was pure coincidence that we managed to unravel the evidence and work out what was really going on in the various locations. Later on tonight we can email your wife and daughter to let them know you are safe. We have to wait until the rest of the criminals have been arrested and then you can tell your family the good news. Tamarai was very worried about you and tried hard to track you down.'

'I can never thank you all enough. You put yourselves in such danger for a total stranger. You are a very kind and caring family. I will never forget this. Never!'

'Rest now, Karthik. You are still exhausted, both emotionally and physically. I am so pleased to see you have started to make such a strong recovery. One of our friends, Satya, is coming over tonight. We did not know if you spoke any English but I am sure that in any case it will be good for you to see a fellow countryman. Satya organises all the research at the Conference Centre and is extremely kind and gentle. I am sure you will get on famously together.'

'Thank you. That is so very kind. My English is not very good, I'm afraid. I understand most things but I don't speak well,' explained Karthik politely.

'On the contrary, Karthik, your English is very good indeed.'

'Mum, would you like anything to eat?' Sandro asked. 'We had a meal together earlier. We didn't know when you would come back and all the excitement, worry and anticipation was making us exceedingly hungry. Even Karthik was hungry!'

Karthik beamed at Sandro and nodded in agreement. He was looking very tired and drawn but Maria was relieved that he was eating and drinking again, albeit in very small quantities.

'Let's wait for Satya,' suggested Maria. 'Then we'll have a snack together. I assume, Sandro, that there is still some food left in the fridge.'

'Of course there is, Mum! I'm not such a gannet as you think I am.'

***

Rafa had waited nervously for over twenty minutes before his surly employer eventually appeared on the quay, grunted a non-committal greeting and climbed aboard the fishing boat. Pedro seemed relatively sober as he started the engine and took up his position of superiority at the helm. It soon became apparent, however, that he had been drinking heavily as usual in one of the many harbour bars. Rafa tried not to think about his drunken blackmailer as he cast off from the quay and coiled up the ropes methodically as usual while they chugged slowly out of the harbour. The sea was calm and the boat made good progress, leaving the bright harbour lights quickly behind them. Rafa tried to comfort himself with the thought that he would never have to do this sort of trip again. Deep in the pit of his stomach, however, he had a ghastly feeling that he might never do any trip again, that this night might indeed be his last. Maria had sent him a very encouraging text to cheer him on his way. He must hold fast to her message, repeat it like a mantra in the hours to come and hope that all would go as planned. She promised they would wait up and had made up a bed ready for him. She did not want him to be on his own after his nerve-racking ordeal. She had reassured Rafa that he was part of their family now more than ever and he would always be safe with them. Thinking about Maria's text had a calming effect on Rafa and he felt more able to cope with the dangers that lay ahead.

Suddenly the Inspector's mobile chirped into life, breaking the gloomy silence in the room. Inspector Rico Martinez listened intently. The Professor was still slumped awkwardly in his chair. One officer was checking data on the computer, while the other worked his way through the filing system, looking for evidence. The Hotel Manager was standing glumly by the window, his wrists handcuffed behind him. He was at a loss to comprehend what was happening. He had come into the Professor's office for their usual fortnightly meeting and had been caught completely off-guard. He had been searched, deprived of his mobile, arrested by three total strangers and accused of being an accessory to murder. All this fuss over two sick Indian hotel guests! They had probably died from some illness; he didn't know and he didn't care; they had certainly not been murdered. Why were these people being so melodramatic? He had looked across to the Professor in sheer disbelief and total dismay. The Professor had, however, avoided his eyes and said not a word. He had just sat there in stunned silence. He was no help whatsoever. The Hotel Manager decided that the Professor's strategy was perhaps wise in the circumstances and it might be best to say nothing that might incriminate either of them. He shifted uncomfortably and wondered wearily how much longer they would have to remain in the cramped office with these three unhelpful strangers. He didn't understand what was happening. He had just obeyed orders. Why was the Professor being such a devious rat? Why didn't the Professor exonerate him and sort things out?

It was a very gloomy, dismal night and nothing seemed to disturb the vast expanse of black undulating ocean. Pedro had obviously drunk far too much before coming onboard. Rafa was worried because his nasty skipper was becoming angrier and more impatient by the minute as they had not yet managed to locate the Africans they were supposed to 'rescue'. After an agonising search Rafa eventually spotted a small rowing-boat about a hundred metres to starboard and pointed it out to Pedro. It looked empty. Rafa's spirits sank. That would be a disaster if the refugees had not survived. Pedro would go berserk. The fishing boat came carefully alongside and Rafa peered desperately into the little boat, willing the refugees to be alive. Oh, the relief which spread through his limbs! The Africans were still alive. They were huddled together below the gunwales and therefore not visible at a distance. Rafa was shaking as he prepared as usual to help the refugees to transfer from their leaky craft to the more seaworthy vessel. There were twelve ragged, half-starved bodies waiting for rescue.

Rafa wondered how many would be allowed to go with them this time. He looked over to his mean and contemptible employer for instructions. Pedro indicated that ten could come aboard on this occasion and picked up the baseball bat in readiness to deter the last two who would inevitably try in desperation to board. Pedro always considered it a waste of bodies and profit not to transfer all the Africans, but he had his instructions and he knew better than to disobey again the very precise orders he had been given. Pedro slammed the engine into reverse, leaving the last two Africans to face the perilous ocean on their own. The fishing boat distanced itself quickly from the small boat and Pedro set his course for La Rajita as usual. Rafa settled the ten new passengers quickly and quietly and handed round the drinks and biscuits he had thoughtfully bought for them. The Africans smiled gratefully at him, whilst Pedro glowered mercilessly from the stern of the vessel and cursed him loudly for 'pampering black vermin.' Rafa took care to stay well away from Pedro and well out of range of the dreaded baseball bat. One more hour before Armageddon. Time was dragging interminably. He would be so glad when this night's work was over.

Having accompanied his 'associates' out of the building without arousing the suspicions of the only Security officer on duty, Satya heaved a sigh of relief. The Security guard had looked up briefly from his paperwork, had recognised Satya, the Professor and the Hotel Manager, bade them all a cursory 'goodnight' and carried on with his paperwork. He had not even noticed that two of the men were handcuffed and he had allowed Satya to sign them all out. Satya had to smile to himself because none of the security precautions and regulations so carefully instituted by the Professor had saved him from being arrested and marched out of the Centre in broad daylight by three strangers. He was relieved that the Professor had not created a scene or begged for help. Satya sent a quick message to Maria and Ana that all had gone according to plan and he was now on his way to their house. Suddenly he felt very hungry and thirsty and realised that it was hours since he had last eaten. He still found it difficult to come to terms with what the Professor had done. Such a heinous crime! Such a callous man! No wonder he had not been remotely interested in the biodiversity and conservation of the Canary Islands. The Conference Centre had just been a cover to conceal his abhorrent activities. Who would have thought that money could corrupt such a brilliant mind and lead him to mastermind such mass slaughter! Satya had studiously avoided looking at the Professor when he had helped escort him down to Reception and out of the Centre. How could one look a murderer in the eyes?

⁂

Ana was waiting outside the cottage for Satya. She rushed into his open arms and they had a few quiet minutes together before joining the family in the sitting-room. Maria introduced Satya first to Felix, who shook his hand and welcomed him warmly into their family home and then to Karthik. The surgeon was obviously delighted to see a fellow countryman and it was not long before the two of them were side by side on the sofa chattering away companionably in their native tongue. Ana and Sandro busied themselves in the kitchen while Maria and Felix exchanged a few anxious words about Rafa. Maria reassured Felix that so far everything had gone well and she had every faith in the Inspector's organisation and execution of the comprehensive plan they had worked out together. They just had to be patient and wait for Rafa to return.

He would certainly need their help and support after an extremely traumatic day.

Juan and the family had just started their evening meal when the telephone rang. Juan listened to the agitated voice on the line and eventually agreed with great reluctance to go back to the hotel after he had eaten. The voice was not to be pacified by this arrangement and insisted he come immediately and they would provide him with a meal but he must come at once. Juan put down the receiver and tried to explain to Sara why he had to return to the hotel straight away, even though he had already done one shift that day. Apparently the Hotel Manager was yet again nowhere to be found and the young inexperienced receptionist was panicking and felt that a senior person ought to be on duty as there were so many guests at the moment. Sara was outraged but realised that there was very little point in protesting, as Juan had already agreed to go. Juan urged the family to continue their meal without him as he stumped upstairs to change back into his uniform. Wretched manager! He was always doing a disappearing act and Juan was left to pick up the pieces. What was the point in employing someone so unreliable in a position of authority? He, Juan, would be more than happy to do the Manager's job permanently, if he were paid properly. He would certainly be much more reliable and not disappear when the mood took him.

They could just about make out the steep jagged cliffs, as they carefully approached La Rajita in the gloomy darkness. Thick cloud obscured any moonlight. The sea was eerily quiet and unusually well-behaved. Just a gentle swell. No wild waves crashing dangerously on to the rocks flinging spray in every direction. Rafa glanced nervously at the luminous dial of his watch. His heart was pounding alarmingly. It felt as though it would jump out of his chest cavity at any moment. His skin was clammy, but he felt chilled to the bone. He felt almost physically sick with dread. He concentrated on willing his hands not to shake. He must keep calm and not betray the terror which threatened to overwhelm him at any moment. He could hardly see the old wooden jetty where they would be landing their precious cargo. Soon his fate would be decided. A few hundred metres . . . .

Maria, Satya and Karthik had enjoyed their meal together. Meanwhile Ana had emailed Tamarai in India with the good news about her father and had received an ecstatic reply from the family despite the time zone difference. Karthik was elated but obviously drained by the emotional trauma. Satya persuaded him to lie down and rest in order to conserve his strength. He promised to visit him again the next day, if the family were happy for him to do so. He could see from the expression on their faces that they would be more than happy for him to visit again. Karthik sank back exhausted into the pillows and was soon snoring rhythmically. Maria motioned to them all to leave the surgeon to sleep. Felix turned out the lights in the sitting-room and joined the others who were gathered round the kitchen table. He put his arm round Maria and congratulated her on everything that had been achieved in such a short time.

'You are amazing, Mum,' said Sandro. 'Please do tell us what the rest of the code means. I know you must have worked it all out.'

'Actually, it was Chano who unscrambled the code. He told us about it this morning on the way to the police station. I'm absolutely no use at cryptic puzzles.'

'It must be the only thing you can't do, Maria,' said Satya in admiration of his colleague.

'Thank you for that, Satya. However, I'm actually rubbish at lots of things!'

'Come on, Mum! Please tell us what it all meant!'

'Patience, Sandro! You may be very upset when I explain it all.' Maria took a deep breath and exhaled slowly.

'Well, here goes! We had already worked out that 'CP' was the charter plane piloted either by 'D' =

Domingo or 'C' = Chano. 'DE' stands for the delegates to the Conference Centre. So if we take the first line of the encrypted email CP + D + NODE + 7FC > TFN 20001204

We get: Charter plane + Domingo + No delegates to Tenerife North (Los Rodeos airport) at 2000hrs on 12th April.'

'What about '7FC' in the code?' queried Felix.

'That's the horrible part,' replied Maria. 'The pilots carried cargo as well sometimes. Domingo always flew full crates of squid to Tenerife, whereas Chano always flew the empty crates back to La Gomera. It was carefully organised that way so that the two pilots would rarely meet up and would be unlikely to compare notes. It was pure chance that they decided to have a holiday together and started wondering about the crates of squid and other discrepancies they had noticed.'

'Right,' said Sandro. 'I see. The '7FC' are seven full crates and the '7EC' are seven empty crates of squid.'

'What does '10AB' mean?' asked Ana.

'Unfortunately, that refers to 'ten African bodies' which were butchered to order to provide the various organs required for specific transplant operations at the clinic.'

'That bonfire that Auntie Sara's boys saw near La Dama! That was actually at La Rajita, wasn't it, Mum? Were they incinerating the remains of the dead Africans?'

'Yes, Sandro. We think those poor refugees met a horrible end. We found evidence of a bonfire when we were down there.'

'How dreadful! How could anyone do that? That's positively barbaric! I can't understand why any human being could do such a terrible thing to another,' said Ana.

'Money, Ana. Money is unfortunately a great incentive,' said Felix. 'The Professor and his partners in crime have made a great deal of money out of this disgusting scam.'

'I think I must be very thick,' interjected Satya, pensively. 'I really don't understand. What exactly have the crates of squid to do with this ghastly crime?'

'That's the really gruesome bit,' explained Maria. 'Pedro took the squid he caught down to the derelict fish processing factory, carefully packed in crates with ice. The two thugs there removed most of the squid, repacked the crates with the various human organs that had been removed from the Africans at the factory, put some more ice and squid on top to fool the Customs Officers in the unlikely event that they examined the cargo. Then they arranged for a courier to take the crates of squid to the airport to be transported eventually to the Clinic in Tenerife. After the organs had been transplanted into the 'fake' Indian delegates, the empty crates were taken back to the airport and left in the hangar beside the charter plane ready for Chano to load up and fly back to La Gomera. Then the whole horrible cycle would begin again.'

Maria concluded her poignant explanation and looked worriedly around the shocked faces in the kitchen. An almost palpable silence settled on the room.

'Who were the couriers?' asked Ana after a while. 'It can't have been the two guards at the factory because they never deviated from their regular routine, as far as we know.'

'Rafa thinks that the Conference Hotel Manager was probably a courier. According to Juan, he was always disappearing at odd times and Juan was grumbling to Rafa the other day that he was constantly being called in to cover the Manager's absence. He has to stand in as Manager but only gets paid porter's wages. Oh dear! I've just remembered! I think Juan will have to work an extra shift tonight, because the Hotel Manager has of course been arrested. I must apologise to him tomorrow. I expect Sara was very cross about it. Juan could run that hotel very efficiently, if only he were given the chance.'

There was silence again for a few minutes before a very subdued Sandro asked:

'Mum, Dad, would you mind if we young ones went down to the harbour for some fresh air and exercise? We've all been cooped up inside all day.'

'Not at all, so long as you don't say anything about my old bones, young Sandro! Dad and I will stay here and wait for Rafa. Go on and enjoy yourselves! Satya, feel free to thump my son if he teases you too much! He will enjoy pushing you to the limit!'

'You do me an injustice, Mother dear! I am rapidly becoming the perfect son.'

'In your dreams, Sandro,' teased his sister. 'Come on, Satya and get to know my perfect brother! It may be an experience even worse than squid!'

Ana, Satya and Sandro went off laughing towards the harbour. Amazed at their resilience Felix gave Maria a hug and then put the saucepan on to make some fresh coffee. It was going to be a long, agonising wait.

Sara's elder son answered the phone and relayed the message to his mother. Apparently the Hotel Manager had not yet returned, so Dad was going to have to stand in until he showed up and didn't know when he would be home. Sara was obviously very annoyed but acknowledged the message in silence. She would talk to Juan tomorrow. This couldn't go on. Juan was becoming very tired and irritable and it was disrupting family life. No employee should have to work double shifts so often. It was all wrong!

Two officers in an unmarked police car had unobtrusively collected the Professor and the Hotel Manager from the Conference Centre and had just arrived with their two taciturn prisoners at the rear of the police station in the capital, San Sebastian. They quickly transferred the handcuffed criminals into separate cells and locked them in securely. Meanwhile the Inspector and two other officers had driven over to La Rajita to join several other policemen already waiting there for the next phase of the operation. The Inspector gathered his men near the old fish factory and went over the operational plan. He explained why precision and accurate timing would be so necessary. He also made it abundantly clear that he would not tolerate any slip-shod actions and that any breach of his instructions would result in severe disciplinary action. At a signal from the Inspector the various groups dispersed and took up their operational positions. The sea was quite calm and not splashing all over the rocks, which was a tremendous advantage. Luck was also on their side, because it was a very cloudy and dark night and it would be much easier to lie in wait in the overcast gloom rather than silhouetted in bright moonlight.

The Professor sat bolt upright on the hard wooden bench in his cell. He had declined the offer of legal representation and continued to bluster that he was innocent of any crime and these stupid fools would severely regret imprisoning him. His arrogance was almost keeping the nightmare at bay. No-one surely would be clever enough to prove that he was guilty. Others were much more guilty than he was. Nothing connected him with the real villains. He thought he had carefully deleted information on his mobile, so it didn't matter that he had contacted Carlos on the landline at the Clinic, when his mobile was not working. Carlos had been absolutely furious that he had used the landline but he just had to talk to him every day. Carlos was the love of his life. If they couldn't be together, he just had to hear his voice. Texting was just not the same. Carlos had been so angry with him and he couldn't understand why. It was the worst four days of their relationship. He had thought they were going to split up and he couldn't bear that thought. Life without Carlos would be intolerable. He could just about cope with the times apart, which seemed to be even longer than before, provided that he had the reassurance that they would be together again soon. He had decided to put a lump sum into the new off-shore account which Carlos had opened recently for certain private transactions. He desperately hoped that it might appease his inexplicable anger and bad temper. The strategy seemed to have worked.

The Professor continued his musings. Any evidence would only be circumstantial at best and no court would convict him on that basis. He was innocent as far as the law was concerned. He could weather a few nasty rumours and any unpleasant scandal would soon die down. Life would eventually return to normal. He and Carlos both had extremely healthy bank balances in various off-shore accounts and could afford to retire gracefully. He would happily retire anywhere with Carlos. Was Carlos ready to retire? They had never discussed it. He had no idea. Perhaps Carlos would like him to do a few lecture tours at prestigious universities in America. That was always a very lucrative proposition. He was after all an excellent lecturer and an eminent academic in his field. He would surely be in demand in the academic world. Perhaps Carlos would find another 'project' for them, perhaps in South America or South Africa. There was still plenty of scope worldwide for similar scams. The authorities in these places were always so lax that it was easy to bamboozle them. Carlos seemed to crave money and power. Yes, he reflected, everything would be fine once he had been released from this stupid humiliating cage. It was a far cry from the expensive and luxurious hotel suites to which he had become accustomed. This was obviously just a temporary setback.

Rafa's pre-arranged signal with the torch was answered almost immediately by the two men on the shore near the factory. Slowly the fishing boat moved into position near the semi-derelict jetty. Rafa jumped ashore as usual and tied up the boat fore and aft with two double half-hitches and an extra granny knot for good measure. It was very dark and fortunately Pedro could not see exactly what he was doing. Then Rafa started to help the ragged Africans to disembark. They were very weak and quite unsteady on their feet. Seven managed to scramble from the boat to the wooden jetty without incident. Then one of them seemed to fall and hurt himself and Rafa had to half drag, half carry the poor man the length of the jetty to put him down on the rocks. Pedro was growing increasingly more impatient and cursing him wildly, telling him to leave that African to rot, get the others off and get back on the boat in the next thirty seconds or he would leave Rafa there and he could walk home. As it was so overcast Pedro was obviously frustrated that he could not really see what Rafa was doing. He heard his usual shout to the Africans of 'Hotel! Hotel!' and could just about see a light flashing on the shore.

Sandro, Ana and Satya were discussing events over soft drinks in a café down by the harbour. Sandro noticed the police launch was not in the harbour and remarked on it to the others. They wondered how that fitted in to the master plan. They were still stunned by the realization of what had been going on in the friendly little island. Ana and Sandro had deliberately played down the horror they felt so as not to alarm Karthik or their parents. They were, however, finding it extremely difficult to come to terms with the reality of the crimes that had been committed only a few kilometres away. Ana and Satya also knew they were now facing unemployment if the Centre closed and worried that they might be separated in the near future. Sandro was still digesting the revelations of the Code and was secretly very grateful that he had not been able to decipher its hidden horrors. Satya was also questioning his preconceived ideas about destiny. The three 'young ones' sat there rather sombrely in the bright café, peering out into the dark night. Even the usually irrepressible Sandro did not have the energy or enthusiasm to tease Satya about 'lizard-hunting.' It was an uncomfortable wait for the final episode, but they found an understanding comradeship together and decided to stay down by the harbour for a while longer. Their parents were probably also grateful for some space to come to terms with the tragic revelations. Who would ever have imagined that such things could happen on La Gomera? They sat in stunned silence, sipping their drinks.

At last a figure reappeared out of the gloom, helped the two remaining Africans to disembark and then climbed back on board. He immediately grabbed the baseball bat and threw it quickly over the side of the boat into the sea. Pedro was taken aback by his employee's peculiar behaviour. He decided that Rafa had gone raving bonkers and advanced menacingly towards him, cursing volubly. He did not, therefore, notice the two men clambering on to the boat behind him. Just as he was about to make violent contact with the fisherman in the prow of the boat, Pedro was grabbed from behind and handcuffed. Pedro started to kick out viciously so they tied his feet together as well and attached them to a solid metal structure on the boat. Trussed up like an oven-ready turkey, Pedro started to scream and shout abuse at his unwelcome visitors.

The fisherman turned round and pointed a rather efficient-looking hand gun in his direction and told him to be silent. The effect was instantaneous. Pedro subsided in total shock. The gun levelled at him was held not by Rafa, as he had assumed, but by someone dressed exactly like Rafa who introduced himself as a very senior policeman. The Inspector informed him that Rafa had already been arrested and taken away for questioning. Meanwhile he and Pedro were going to have a nice cosy chat about trafficking African immigrants who were subsequently murdered and incinerated. The preliminary enquiry was going to take place on the boat and would be recorded and documented by the two officers who were now sitting on either side of him. Pedro, totally bewildered and confused, looked from one to the other. Escape was out of the question. Was he going to be tortured and then shot? Were these really policemen or had the 'Boss' decided to eliminate him and had sent some henchmen to do his dirty work again? Surely not! Pedro was a vital part of the whole scam. Pedro was important. Pedro was required as skipper, courier and taxi-driver. Nothing would work without him. Pedro was absolutely essential to the success of this lucrative trade. Who could have betrayed him? Not Rafa, that was certain. Rafa was stupid and knew virtually nothing of the scam and anyway he had just been arrested, so that ruled him out. The Professor? No, he made far too much money out of this African trade and would want to keep it running. That left the Hotel Manager, the 'Boss' and those two nasty creeps at the factory. When Pedro eventually discovered who had betrayed him, he would take the necessary steps to remove him from the planet. Pedro would show no mercy! Comforted by the thought of future revenge, Pedro relaxed a little but was jolted back into harsh reality by the Inspector's questions about his bank account and his mobile phone. Pedro indicated meekly that his mobile was in the back pocket of his jeans and one of the policemen rapidly collected it and started to investigate the contacts and other data listed on the phone. Pedro was becoming increasingly alarmed as it slowly began to infiltrate his lazy and befuddled brain cells that certain information on his mobile could in fact incriminate him, if the police investigated too closely. He vaguely remembered the 'Boss' instructing him to delete everything immediately. Of course, Pedro had been far too lazy to bother.

'Bingo, Sir!' said the officer who was fiddling with the mobile. 'The numbers tally perfectly and there are also plenty of incriminating text messages with instructions for rendezvous times at sea, times to deliver crates of squid to the factory and times to deliver crates to the airport for onward transfer.'

Suddenly the officer turned pale and looked as if he were going to be violently sick.

'Sorry, Sir,' apologised the officer. 'There is also a message here about collecting bits of bodies to feed to the whales and dolphins to keep them happy and preserve the supply of squid because it was too windy to have a bonfire to dispose of the remains.'

'What a charming fisherman you are!' said the Inspector in a sarcastic tone. 'Well, now that we have established your guilt beyond any possible doubt, perhaps we can discuss what we are going to do with you.'

Pedro could not stop the trembling in his limbs. Abject animal fear threatened to overwhelm him. He wished that he had not had so much to drink down at the harbour bar. He felt he was going to be violently sick. He was bound hand and foot to the winch in his own boat and was powerless to intervene in the scene which was unfolding with frightening certainty around him. If they were policemen, why didn't they just arrest him and take him in to the police station? He could easily bribe them there or bribe a clever lawyer and lay the blame squarely on someone else. He had just obeyed orders, so he couldn't be guilty of any crime. He had bribed and bulldozed his way so many times out of problems in the past. On the other hand, if they weren't policemen, who on earth were they? More importantly, what were they going to do next? Were they going to murder him and take his boat? Could he bargain the boat for his life? He had enough money in the bank for a pleasant retirement. He could leave this squid job alone and just concentrate on the taxi business. That was also comparatively easy money. As Pedro turned over this strategy in his mind, the man with the gun spoke to him again.

Felix came back into the kitchen to report that Karthik seemed to be sleeping soundly.

'He must be too exhausted even to have nightmares,' said Felix to his wife.

'I expect he will have nightmares for the rest of his life, poor man,' replied Maria. 'I am glad he has found some peace here to recover a little from the horrible things which have happened to him in the last few weeks. He seems to be a very kind and gentle soul with a great vision for helping the poorest people in his homeland, who have no access to health care. He must have felt so angry and humiliated at being exploited in that Clinic. I cannot begin to imagine what he felt when he had to work at gunpoint in such terrible conditions in the fish factory. I don't know how he had the inner strength to survive that. It's also going to be very gruelling for him to give evidence to the police, when he feels strong enough, but I'm sure that he will face it bravely with calm dignity. It will be a kind of catharsis. Hopefully he will feel very relieved afterwards when all the questioning is over and his horrible ordeal will not be quite so vivid.'

'I think it will be quite a while before he is physically strong enough to fly back to India. I keep telling him that he is welcome to stay for as long as he wants. We are pleased to have him here, although it is a bit crowded!'

'We'll manage!' said Maria, smiling. 'I wonder how 'the young ones' are coping. I think the revelations have shocked them deeply, though they are trying hard not to show it. I do hope Sandro isn't teasing them tonight. He can be rather insensitive sometimes.'

'Ana will keep him in order, never fear!'

At that moment there was a sharp knock on the door. Maria and Felix froze. They knew it wasn't the three 'young ones' as Sandro had christened them. Felix recovered first and went off to see who was calling so late at night. It certainly wasn't Rafa.

More officers arrived back at the police station, having released the two ruthless thugs in the old fish factory from their improvised metal cage only to re-imprison them in the cage in the rear of the police van. They were very subdued, dirty, smelly and rather hungry and thirsty, but otherwise well able to face the interrogation planned by the Inspector for the next day. They were put into the same cell for the night. Never had the police station been so busy! The policemen on duty made sure that everything was in order. They had no desire to incur the wrath of their superior officer. He had already sent four of their colleagues off for 'retraining and reassessment' and they had no inclination to join them. Their comfortable life-style had been severely disrupted by the arrival of this new Inspector. He had vociferously condemned their slap-dash methods and voiced strident disapproval of the culture of bribes and favours which permeated the local police force. His belligerent tone brooked no argument. They bitterly resented his intrusion but were slowly setting about the gigantic task of 'cleaning up their act' and 'serving the community in a professional and impartial manner as befitted a modern police force.' Initial resentment had given way to the stark realization that their jobs were now far from secure. The Inspector was unfortunately here to stay and had every intention of dragging them kicking and screaming into line. His preliminary investigations had opened up several cans of worms and many more would be wriggling and squirming if the Inspector continued with his 'spring-clean', as he liked to call it. The surprise arrest of that nasty duplicitous lawyer, Mendosa, had left many of them extremely uncomfortable and anxious. He could easily incriminate so many of them and would probably do so, if he thought it would save his own skin.

The ten African refugees had been dropped off at the small local medical centre for an initial health and welfare assessment. They would be transferred in due course in a police van by ferry to Tenerife for 'asylum processing.' They would never know how lucky they were to escape the fate of their fellow countrymen who had been 'rescued' during the previous months and taken to the fish factory for a different sort of processing.

Sandro could just make out the police launch coming back into the harbour, closely followed by Pedro's fishing boat. He alerted his sister and Satya and their gaze was riveted on the harbour entrance. The harbour lights made little impression, however, on the insidious darkness and it was impossible to see clearly what was happening. A group of people seemed to have scrambled on to the quay and gathered near the police launch. They had expected noise and confused shouting but it was ominously quiet. They continued to watch as three vehicles drew up and the group on the quayside organised itself for onward transport. The cars departed unobtrusively and the three 'young ones' in the cafe were left wondering whether the police operation had been successful or not. Certainly, they had not witnessed anything conclusive down at the harbour. In the pervasive gloom they could not recognise any of the figures and did not know whether Pedro and Rafa had been amongst the passengers in the two boats. They sipped their drinks in rather glum silence, preoccupied with thoughts of all the people involved in the day's events.

One car diverted to the nearby medical centre to drop off the two other Africans who had been left for dead by Pedro in the leaky rowing boat. With the help of Rafa's directions the police launch had eventually managed to locate and rescue them. They were dehydrated and terrified, but otherwise in reasonable condition. They had been fortunate that the sea had been calm. Another police car had headed straight to the police station in San Sebastian to discharge its unpleasant cargo into the remaining empty cell. The third car had stopped a few hundred metres from the harbour to discharge other urgent business.

Five weeks later. Playa de Santiago, La Gomera, Canary Islands

'It's really strange here without Karthik, isn't it, Mum?'

'Yes, Ana. It certainly is! He was like one of the family. I know he only stayed in the cottage a few days before he moved over to that lovely suite in the Conference Hotel near Satya. I'm sure that he was much more comfortable there! It would certainly be less crowded than here and it was good for him to have Satya so close,' said Maria.

'Yes, it was,' agreed Ana. 'I know that the hotel staff spoilt him rotten and at least he didn't have to put up with Sandro teasing him all the time! He's made a steady recovery these last few weeks and we did see him almost every day. It was lovely that he felt well enough yesterday to start the journey back to India. His family will be overjoyed.'

'Yes, I'm sure they can't wait to see him again. He has promised to keep in touch and wants us to go and visit him and his family, though there's not much chance of that. At least he now has some happy memories of our Islands to try to obliterate his nightmarish ordeal. The Indian government paid all of his hotel and repatriation expenses so he did not need to worry on that score. He is apparently very highly thought of in India and has been offered a very prestigious position as Director of Surgery when he is well enough to take it. It is in a new Medical Centre near Chennai where he will be able to treat everyone, rich and poor, so he will be able to fulfil his dream after all. He is such a kind and gentle person with a lovely sense of humour. I'm glad that he and Satya enjoyed each other's company so much. Fancy them both coming from the same region! It must have eased the homesickness for him a little.'

'I'm sure he can hardly wait to be reunited with his family. Satya says he hasn't told them anything yet about his ordeal, just that he has been ill and is recovering slowly.'

'I think the Indian government asked him to keep everything as low-key as possible in order to preserve the integrity of the Centre. As far as Satya knows, the Conference Centre and the Hotel are going to be kept open, so everyone's job is secure.'

'I hear that Juan is enjoying his new position as Manager at the Hotel,' added Felix. 'Apparently, he had to step in so often to cover when the proper Manager was 'otherwise engaged' that he can do the job quite automatically now. He works much more regular hours too, so Sara is happier and he only does night shifts if a real emergency arises.'

'Auntie Sara must be much happier,' said Sandro, 'because she has let Cisco and Cesar go camping for a whole week in the Garajonay forest!'

'Good for her,' interjected Ana. 'They are good kids and pretty responsible, considering they're male!'

'You're treading on very thin ice, sis, with comments like that! Don't tell me you didn't have the occasional irresponsible moment in your far-off younger days!'

The cushion flew across the room and landed softly on the floor, just missing her brother who had managed to duck at the right moment. Sandro flopped down on the sofa and joined in the general laughter.

'Mum, do you know yet what exactly happened to the Hotel Manager and what part he played in the scam?'

'Well, Rafa was right in his assumption that he was also a 'courier'. That made him an accessory to the crime. He was being blackmailed apparently for some mistake he had made in the past in India and could therefore be easily manipulated. I don't know if he knew exactly what was going on or if he just chose to ignore it. Anyway, he was unofficially deported to India for the authorities there to deal with him.'

'Has your friendly Inspector Rico Martinez told you yet what happened to the Professor in the end? He just seems to have disappeared,' said Ana.

'Yes and no. He phoned this morning. As you know, the Professor was held in the cells at San Sebastian for several days and interrogated in depth. He refused point blank to have any legal representation because he still insisted he was innocent of any crime and had just tried to help some Indian colleagues. However, he eventually confessed to almost everything when confronted by all the evidence. He also gave the authorities access to his bank accounts and his ill-gotten gains have been confiscated under the 'Proceeds of Crime' legislation. Apparently, there may perhaps be insufficient evidence according to Rico to secure a conviction, as so much of the evidence is purely circumstantial. He did not tell the Professor that, of course. He kept him guessing about the possible outcome. In the end a deal was struck with the Indian government, because they did not want any scandal about the Centre. The Professor was discreetly transferred to a village near Santa Cruz on Tenerife under house-arrest somewhere safe and eventually deported to India last week where, in return for his 'freedom', he will face very severe restrictions. He is not allowed to leave India under ANY circumstances, not even for a lecture tour; he is forbidden to own or use a computer; all his movements and contacts will be strictly monitored and he must report weekly to the local police station. If he infringes any of the conditions imposed on him, the Indian and Spanish authorities have threatened him that they will not hesitate to imprison him at once and put him on trial for murder. It is very much in his own interests to keep quiet and behave, if he wants to stay a free man. His flamboyant lifestyle will be severely restricted but otherwise I think he has escaped very lightly indeed.'

'He should be hung, drawn and quartered in my opinion,' said Ana hotly. 'He never got his hands dirty, but he nevertheless caused the death of lots of innocent people and he should pay for it. He was evil.'

'You're right of course, Ana,' said Felix, sadly. 'Unfortunately, when political expedience comes into the equation, justice is never done. The Professor will hopefully never be in a position again to commit such a crime. When you are trying to hush up a potentially devastating scandal for the benefit of future gains, it is always a delicate balancing act. The outcome is not at all what we think the Professor deserved but from the purely selfish point of view of the locals, it is much better if the whole sordid business is played down and the Conference Centre and Hotel remain operational. There is nothing to be gained by publicising what happened; it will only damage tourism and everyone's livelihood here. Everyone involved is therefore keeping a low profile. As far as the locals are concerned, the Professor and the Hotel Manager have had to return to India for personal reasons. Juan has already taken over as Manager of the Hotel and a new Director of the Conference Centre will be appointed in due course.

Meanwhile, Satya is, as you know, working very hard to hold the fort.'

'It also means that Domingo and Chano will still have a job here as charter pilots and don't have to return to Spain to look for work,' added Sandro. 'That's great news, as far as I'm concerned. I love their wicked sense of humour! We have had some good times with them in the last few weeks, haven't we? Chano has even offered to let me sit in the cockpit with him and observe him flying the plane, if I do some study first!'

'He's optimistic! My brother studying! I'd better warn Chano that he will have to wait a very, very long time!'

Before Sandro could reach the cushion to hurl at his sister, his phone rang and he hastened to answer it.

Satya was exhausted. In desperation, he had contacted the various Indian Government Departments yet again and threatened to resign unless they acted on his suggestions in the very near future. He knew only too well that speedy decision-making was definitely not their strong point but after almost six weeks of debate, argument and negotiation, something should surely have been achieved. Even with Ana's invaluable help, he had realized very quickly that he could not run the Centre as it should be run and manage all the research and development as well. The new Director was yet to be appointed and would not be in post for at least another six months and even then they would need someone efficient during the transition period to run the administration side of the Centre to ensure continued sponsorship and development funds. Everything had slipped very badly under the reign of the Professor and a great deal needed to be re-organised if the Centre were to fulfil its remit. The Government appeared very eager to continue to develop the work of the Centre but seemed unable to take any decisive action to secure its future. Satya kept emphasising that the Centre was a flagship enterprise for India and he failed to understand why the authorities could not be more proactive. He had explained to them yet again that delay in future planning would endanger the very viability of the Centre. His frustration had been gnawing away slowly at him and he had even discussed with Ana the previous evening the unpleasant possibility of leaving the Centre and considering jobs elsewhere, much to her evident dismay and consternation.

Hence his ultimatum this morning! Much to his amazement and relief, he had just received an email from the Research and Development Department confirming that he could offer the position of Centre Administrator to Maria and also make Ana's position permanent. He would ring Maria straight away. He hoped that she would accept the job. She was the perfect candidate and would run the Centre very efficiently and intelligently, leaving him to deal with the Research and Development side. After an unpleasantly hectic few weeks, he would be able to relax and enjoy his job again. He would be able to continue to work with Ana, the love of his life. He wanted Ana to study and follow her dream and not be chained to a mundane office job. At least she would have financial security now and that would enable her to study part-time or full-time, if that was what she wanted. They had discussed several options over the past weeks. Ana was, however, still deeply shocked at the transplant scandal and would need time to make decisions about her future. He would support her in whatever she decided to do. He absolutely adored her. He wanted to spend the rest of his life with her, but did not want to pressurise her in any way. He decided to contact Maria first and then tell Ana the good news when she returned from her errand at the Conference Hotel.

Sandro jumped nimbly ashore and tied up the boat securely, ready for the day-trippers to disembark. It had been another successful expedition along the coast and the dolphins had behaved impeccably! Some of the tourists had taken amazing photos which would no doubt be posted online and enhance the reputation of their boat trips even further. Free advertising! He was really enjoying the work and the company and after lengthy discussions with all concerned, he had taken two important decisions. He was going to study part-time and gain higher qualifications in Maths, Physics and English. He would work part-time during the week as guide on the boat trips and as a taxi-driver at the weekends in order to pay for the flying lessons he wanted to have. Eventually, he hoped to become an airline pilot like Chano, who was such a great inspiration. If it turned out that he had no real aptitude for flying, then he would take over the taxi business and run that. Thank goodness he had bothered to learn to drive. Why had he been so incredibly lazy and directionless as a teenager? He was lucky he had a chance to make up for lost time. At least now if he studied and worked hard, he would have improved his mind and tried to expand his horizons and done something useful with his life. It was wonderful that his parents had been allowed to take over the taxi business from the absent Pedro. The other driver had been kept on and they all worked amicably together, sharing the work and thus avoiding long hot shifts.

Uncle Pedro's boat was still languishing in the harbour. Sandro hoped that no-one locally would buy it and set up in competition to them. It was a bigger and better boat and they would have liked to buy it but it would be much too expensive. It would certainly be more profitable than theirs. Time would tell! Sandro felt very settled now and didn't want anything to 'rock the boat.' As soon as that thought crossed his mind, Sandro had to laugh at his own silly inadvertent pun. At the sound of laughter Felix and Rafa looked up from the stern of the boat where they were working. Felix was delighted to see his son and his best friend so happy and settled. The three of them worked well together and it was a happy ship.

Rafa could still not believe his good fortune. He had heard last week that he was not going to be prosecuted for his unwitting role in the scandal, because he had done so much to retrieve the situation. Neither the Indian nor the Spanish government wanted the Professor's case to come to court. For totally different reasons, they had hushed up the whole horrible affair and life had continued quietly on the Islands. Pedro was out of his life for ever. How wonderful was that! With Pedro had gone the fear, the guilt, the threats, the sleepless nights and the desperate days. His life had changed forever and he was so happy and healthy now. He knew he would never be able to repay the kindness and friendship of Maria and Felix. He owed them his life and his happiness and would do anything he could for them.

Maria was expecting a phone call from Sara and picked up the phone rather absent-mindedly when it rang. She suddenly realized that it was in fact Satya on the phone and had to ask him to repeat what he had just said. She apologised profusely that she had not been concentrating. Satya just laughed and repeated the job offer to her, emphasising that he really wanted her to accept the position and sort out the problems at the Centre. Maria was taken aback that the Indian government were offering her a job at all, never mind the generosity of the terms and conditions of such a prestigious position.

'Why me? I'm only the cleaner there. I haven't even applied for the job,' stammered Maria. 'They don't know anything about me.'

'On the contrary,' replied Satya. 'I have told them a lot about you and have recommended you for the position and your friend, Inspector Rico, fully endorsed your appointment. He said you were the most meticulous and organised person he had ever come across and they would be foolish not to employ you. He said he wanted to employ you himself, but the budget would not allow it. He was very persuasive and has been in regular contact with the Indian departments concerned. Please say 'yes', Maria! I really need you and your organisational skills here. I'm going under rapidly. I'm an academic. I haven't a clue about the day-to-day running of an organisation. I'm totally, utterly and completely useless at it. You could do it all so easily and efficiently. It would be a great pleasure and a bonus to have you working here.'

'What about Ana? She might not appreciate having me around.'

'I don't think she will have any objections. I think she will be very pleased for you and be very supportive. She doesn't know yet, but her job has been made permanent, so she has financial security and can take her time making decisions about the future. In any case, she will be helping me with admin for the research and development which is expanding and organising conferences and lecturers, whereas you will be dealing with financial matters, marketing, sponsorship and general day-to-day running of the Centre. You will have your own office and clerical staff so you won't really be working closely together. She's at the Hotel at the moment, sorting out some paperwork for me. Would you like to come up to the Centre now, Maria and we can all discuss it together? Ana should be back shortly and I promise not to say a word until you are here.'

'Yes,' replied Maria, dazed by the unexpected turn of events. 'That sounds a good idea. Thank you, Satya, for your faith in my ability. I'm flattered and totally bemused.'

'My pleasure, Maria. You deserve a position like this. From a very selfish point of view, you will make my life so much easier and I know you will be perfect for the Centre!'

'What happens when the new Professor is appointed? I would be rather surplus to requirements then.'

'Actually, I have just been informed that they aren't going to appoint a new Professor. They want a different format this time. They want the Centre to be much more research-based and there will be visiting lecturers for the various conferences. I just heard this morning. They have also offered me a new contract for five years as Director of Research and Development and I may stipulate the projects we want to work on. I can't quite believe it. This morning I was so frustrated with their indecision that I was ready to resign and a few hours later I have been offered everything I wanted—you, Ana and the freedom for research and no new boss to worry about. We report directly to the government. It's incredible!'

'That's marvellous news, Satya. Congratulations. I'm on my way. See you soon!'

Down by the harbour Rafa, Felix and Sandro were enjoying a well-earned drink in the late afternoon sunshine. They listened attentively as Sandro outlined his plans for the future and wished him every success.

'I hope your aerial navigation is better than your navigation at sea!' Rafa teased him. 'You might never find the runway and have to fly round the Islands in circles until you run out of fuel and then have to ditch in the sea!'

'Come on, Rafa. I'm not that bad! It's only when it's foggy or dark that I haven't a clue where I am!'

'Let's hope you are always flying in good weather during daylight hours!' laughed Felix.

'I'm very pleased for you, Sandro. I'm sure that you'll make a good pilot after a few hundred lessons! Personally, I'll just stick to the ferry if I want to visit one of the other Islands,' teased Rafa.

'Has Chano warned Air Traffic Control and all the Emergency Services that you will be in the air with him next week? Once you have your pilot's licence you'll even be able to pop over to Venezuela and see Uncle Pedro!' added Felix, grinning at his son.

'I never want to see Uncle Pedro again, Dad. I can't believe they didn't imprison him and throw away the key. He knew exactly what was happening and just didn't care.'

'I agree,' said Rafa. 'I never want to see him again either. I'm just glad he agreed to go to Venezuela and leave us in peace. He is not allowed to set foot here or in any EU country again or he will be arrested and tried for murder. Life is so pleasant here without Pedro. I thought he would be the death of me and I am so grateful to still be alive.'

'We're both quite glad you're still around, Rafa! You're really quite good company and very useful on the boat at times!' Sandro playfully moved his chair just out of range of his friend, as he continued to tease him.

'I don't think our Pedro had a lot of choice! The Venezuelan government was so pleased to have the two violent thugs from the factory back in their jurisdiction that they kindly agreed to take Pedro as well, or so I understand! On a more serious note, the police did confiscate all the monies in Pedro's bank account and in the accounts of the others,' said Felix. 'The authorities used that money to buy a one-way ticket to Venezuela for Pedro and they gave him just five hundred euros of 'working capital'. That means Pedro will have to work long and hard in Venezuela in order to survive. So, at least he didn't profit from his criminal activities either. If he misbehaves in any way, he will be dealt with severely, perhaps imprisoned. That's the threat anyway! I don't think we shall ever have the pleasure of Pedro's company again. I know he is my brother, but he has never behaved like a brother to me. In fact, he has been so nasty to so many people for so long, that I think he actually deserves this punishment.'

'No punishment would ever have fitted that terrible crime,' responded Rafa. 'You couldn't imagine that such atrocities could be committed nowadays and that so many people were willing to profit from the misfortune of others.'

'It's interesting that the two thugs turned out to be wanted criminals in Venezuela, so it was easy to extradite them. They didn't profit from their activities either and I hope they both spend a very long time in prison. They were seriously nasty.'

At that moment Felix's mobile rang. He picked it up, managed to press the right button for once and listened intently to his wife's news. Felix was obviously delighted at what he was hearing and was quick to congratulate Maria and Ana on their appointments. He ended the call and hastened to tell Sandro and Rafa the good news. Rafa was so pleased for all of them that he immediately ordered another round of drinks to celebrate.

The Inspector stood up and stretched his weary body. He had been sitting at his office desk for hours, gazing somewhat vacantly into space, hoping for inspiration. He had been going over and over all the paperwork relating to 'the Squid Scandal', as he had named it. Something didn't quite add up. It was all too simplistic, far too neat and tidy. Maria, her family and friends had done a most amazing job and had managed to link apparently totally unconnected events into a revealing sequence and solve a horrible crime, despite the limited resources and information available to them. He was full of admiration for what they had achieved. He thought it highly unlikely that the dunderheads currently employed in the local police force would ever have unearthed the facts lurking behind the evil at La Rajita. Several of them were currently on retraining programmes and had been threatened with dismissal if they didn't buck up their ideas. The staff had all been very 'laid back' when he arrived. Some had almost been horizontal! Things had however changed dramatically. Many of them were obviously very worried not only about their future careers but also about any revelations that suave and nasty lawyer, Diego Mendosa, might make about their activities in the past. There had obviously been serious irregularities and probably bribery involved.

The Inspector decided that he would visit that particular rat later on and have another interrogation session. He currently had Mendosa under house arrest, pending further investigation. Rico could not legally hold him in custody because his alleged crime was fraud and tax evasion. He was not, therefore, in theory at least, any threat to the general public, although his criminal scams had already led to two suicides. Rico had nevertheless taken the precaution of confiscating his passport, money, mobile and all his car keys just in case he managed to evade the police guard. He was an extremely slippery customer and deserved to be prosecuted. He didn't want Mendosa escaping before they had managed to investigate everything fully and secure irrefutable evidence for a conviction and hopefully for a long prison sentence. Scum like Mendosa who bent the law at every opportunity for their own personal gain should not be allowed to practise. Rico wanted him permanently out of circulation before anyone else was driven to desperate measures. He wondered if plea-bargaining of some sort might persuade Mendosa to reveal some interesting facts about some of his activities and associates on the Canary Islands.

He knew that Mendosa was guilty as hell, but there was still a mountain of paperwork to sift through before he could prove it beyond reasonable doubt and put him away for a long time. He wished that he could employ Maria, even on a temporary basis, to help him check through all the paperwork. Unfortunately, he had blown most of the budget on retraining the lacklustre staff he had inherited and thus inadvertently deprived himself of Maria's vital help. He wondered if she had accepted the top administration job at the Centre, for which he had highly recommended her. He would ring her later. He always enjoyed their chats. He wished he had married someone warm and loving like Maria. Instead his marriage had been an unmitigated disaster. Eventually after a very acrimonious divorce he had turned to work for consolation. Now he was a confirmed workaholic and a miserable tyrant! He expected high standards and would not tolerate laziness of any sort. He knew that he was deeply unpopular but it didn't bother him in the slightest. Once the force was operating efficiently and correctly, he would ease up a little and show his nicer side. Meanwhile, back to the grindstone! An enormous heap of paperwork awaited him.

Satya had just finished making coffee for three when Ana and Maria arrived together.

'Perfect timing as always!' Satya grinned as he put the cups of coffee on a tray. His desk was submerged under piles of paperwork so they adjourned to the Professor's office to have their coffee in peace. He told Ana the news that her job was permanent for as long as she wanted it to be. She nearly spilt her coffee in her excitement. Then he told her about the job he had offered her mother and what it would involve.

'Congratulations, Mum! That's wonderful news. You are perfect for that job.'

'Won't it make it difficult for you, Ana, if I accept the job? I don't want to cramp your style,' said Maria with a smile.

'Not at all! It will be lovely working together. I won't be here for ever, anyway. You'll love it here! It's a lovely place to work now that the Professor has gone. You deserve an intelligent job like this. Mum,' added Ana generously.

'I'm glad that's all decided then,' laughed Satya. 'Can you start on Monday, Maria?'

'Shall we celebrate with some of Mum's chocolate cake?'

Without waiting for an answer, Ana skipped off cheerfully down the corridor. What wonderful news! This really was cause for celebration.

The Inspector was still puzzling over the paperwork in front of him. Something vital was eluding him. It could be crucial to the 'Squid Scandal' investigation but he was far too tired to work methodically through the miscellaneous piles of paperwork festering on his desk. He wanted to put this particular scandal to bed as soon as possible. He did not want to waste valuable time on it, as there was not going to be a formal prosecution. He also wanted to devote more energy and resources to the Mendosa case which was proving to be very complex.

The Professor might have been the brains behind the whole operation but Rico believed that there was someone else in the shadows controlling them all like puppets. That obnoxious fisherman, Pedro, kept asking if it had been the 'Boss' who had betrayed him. At first, Rico had just assumed that he was referring to the Professor, but it became clear in the course of the interrogation that Pedro meant someone else. It was someone he had never met. Pedro had received several nasty intimidating phone calls from him. He was clearly absolutely terrified of this man, whoever he might be. The 'Boss' was male and Spanish-speaking, but not from the Canary Islands. That was all Pedro could tell him. The Professor had clearly been taken by surprise when questioned about the 'Boss' but he had quickly denied any knowledge of him. Rico had been unable, even under considerable duress, to extract any more information from the wily academic. Rico reasoned, therefore, that if the Professor were willing to take the blame for everything, he must either be absolutely terrified of the 'Boss' or he would be paid later very handsomely for his silence. Perhaps the Professor was being blackmailed by the 'Boss' as he had blackmailed others? That would indeed be ironic!

'Blackmail! Bank transactions! Money! That was the key. It had to be,' mused the Inspector aloud. He rummaged around the files on his desk and retrieved three he wanted. He thought he had gone through every file but he had obviously not been methodical enough, because the case was never going to court, much to his disgust. He wanted everything done to the letter of the law, but he had been overruled by the politicians in this instance, who understandably wanted to keep so much under wraps.

Perhaps he wasn't looking for the right items? Perhaps he wasn't asking the right questions? He was so tired. He must concentrate. Who was this 'Boss' and where was he based? He carefully laid out the bank statements of the Professor, Pedro, the Hotel Manager and the two Venezuelan thugs from the fish factory. He groaned aloud. It would take hours to cross-reference this lot. If only he could afford to employ Maria or Ana. They were both so meticulous and would quickly recognise discrepancies and reconcile all the accounts.

He decided to phone Maria and ask for her help. He was only too aware that it wasn't strictly ethical, but it was the only way he was going to solve the mystery in the near future. He could take them all out to dinner to express his gratitude. Maria might well refuse in the circumstances, but there was no harm in asking. He dialled her mobile number and waited anxiously.

'Yes, of course, we'll try to help you,' said Maria, without hesitation. 'Would you like to come over this evening and we'll make a start? Or would you rather come tomorrow morning? This is the second job offer I've had today, by the way. I must be doing something right!'

'I hope you accepted the first offer, Maria. As you know, I'd love to have you on my team here, but there is not enough money in the kitty.'

'That's kind of you, Rico. I'll always help you if I can. I am so grateful to you for believing our improbable tale and acting so quickly to arrest the criminals involved and then liaising with the Indian Government so well. And you were so kind to our lovely friend, Rafa. To answer your question! Yes, I did accept the job. I was amazed at the offer. I hope I can cope with everything it involves.'

'I have every confidence in your abilities and so has Satya. If *you* can't cope, then no-one else could! I hope you'll find the position very rewarding.'

'Thank you, Rico. I hope so too. It will certainly be better than working as a cleaner! Have you eaten yet? Would you like to join us for supper? There's plenty to go round. Then we'll see what we can do to help you with the paperwork.'

'That sounds wonderful, but on one condition. I insist on taking you all out to dinner one evening this week. My treat. It's the least I can do to thank you. All this help will be very unofficial, by the way. I don't like to admit it, but I am breaking all my own rules!'

'Understood! No problem, Rico! See you soon!'

The Inspector felt almost rejuvenated at the thought of spending the evening with Maria and her family, even though they would be working through piles of boring bank statements. And another night out with them in the week, too! At least he could avoid Mendosa this evening. He found interviewing him very depressing, because the duplicitous lawyer always had such a slick answer ready for every question. He instinctively knew that Diego Mendosa was lying in every syllable he uttered. He also realized that the devious lawyer was playing with him and taking a sadistic pleasure in trying to thwart him and pervert the course of justice. He would, however, persevere. He would catch him out one day and rid society of one more corrupt creep. Rico gathered up the 'Squid Scandal' files and put them in a large shopping bag. He decided that his briefcase would look rather too official. He locked the Mendosa files in the office safe and headed cheerfully towards his car.

'This sounds exciting, Mum! Helping a real live detective solve a mystery!'

'Actually, it will be quite boring, Sandro. We have to cross-reference all the documents very methodically to try to link all the criminals together. And remember you can't breathe a word about this to anyone. It's all unofficial and highly sensitive material, so we must be careful!'

'No problem! My lips are sealed.'

'That'll be a first!' said his sister. 'You've never been quiet for more than five minutes. You are always talking or whistling or even worse, singing.'

Before Sandro could think of a suitable retort, there was a knock at the cottage door. Maria hastened to welcome the Inspector and led him and the bulging shopping bag through to the kitchen where the table was laid ready.

The meal was very merry and Rico was obviously relaxing and enjoying himself. He accepted Sandro's teasing very good-naturedly and joined in the happy family banter. It was with considerable reluctance that Rico explained what he needed them to do. The table was cleared and work began in earnest. Rico gave Felix the Hotel Manager's bank statements. Sandro took Pedro's records. He himself had the joint account of the two thugs at the fish factory. He gave Maria the Professor's pile and gave Ana blank sheets of paper. She was responsible for noting down any substantial amounts of money and dates of transactions which were otherwise unaccounted for. As Maria called out each transaction, it was duly initialled on the relevant statement. Progress was very slow at first, but eventually they got into a sort of rhythm and the stubborn heap of paperwork gradually diminished.

'Do you realize Sandro is flying with me next week! I offered to let him sit in and observe. I'm sure no-one will mind. He seems very keen to learn to fly,' said Chano, sipping his beer in a café near his tiny apartment.

'Have you checked your life insurance?' Domingo asked, laughing loudly. 'Sandro's a good kid. I hope he takes to flying and works hard to get his pilot's licence. Has he ever flown before?'

'No, never. He's very excited. I'd better put the sick bags handy, just in case!'

'Knowing Sandro, he'll be talking too much to have time to be sick!'

'I hope so! I'm glad our jobs here are safe. In fact, if that government tourism contract comes off as well, we're going to be busier then ever! I rather like these Islands now and want to stay. We've had such a lot of fun these last few weeks with Sandro's family and Rafa. We're all great friends now. It's like being part of an extended family. Who would have thought that our weird adventure on La Gomera would lead where it has?'

'I'm very relieved we can't tell anyone about it. No-one would believe the strange things that happened, so it's just as well that it's all top secret.'

'It doesn't seem right though that only the two thugs were banged up in prison for such a horrible crime. No-one else! Apparently, those guards in the factory had already murdered two other Indian surgeons, who had refused to comply with their demands. It's a great shame we couldn't have accidentally shot them, while we had the chance. We would have done mankind a considerable favour. Scum like that don't deserve a life.'

'You're right, but there would have been even more explaining to do and it was bad enough as it was! I think we rescued Karthik in the nick of time. I don't think he could have held out much longer in that hell-hole. The memory of him in that building amongst those horrible bits of blood spattered bodies will haunt us forever.'

'You're right. By the way, Sandro sent me a text this afternoon to tell me that Karthik was on his way back to India at last. I hope he can put the whole nasty business behind him and look forward to his new job and spending time with his family.'

'I hope so, too. He is one of the good guys. Fancy another beer?'

'Well done, all of you! That would have taken me weeks to do at the station,' said Rico.

'That was fun,' laughed Sandro. 'We managed quite a turn of speed in the end!'

'Can we try to sort out some of the transactions that we haven't matched up?' asked Ana, doing her efficient secretary bit.

'By all means,' replied Rico. 'I didn't want to outstay my welcome and bore you all. Let's see what is still unaccounted for. Over to you, Ana!'

'Well, Uncle Pedro pays out six hundred and fifty euros on the 30th of each month and receives three hundred and sixty euros on the 1st of each month.'

'That's probably Rafa's wages,' said Felix. 'Poor Rafa! How could he manage on that?'

'Have you reference numbers for those transactions, Ana?' queried Rico.

'Yes. 832157 for the wages and 394162 for the other amount.'

'Good Heavens! That's *my* bank account number,' said Felix. 'I pay the rent in every month to that account! All these years I've been paying Pedro, while he's been living rent-free in the farmhouse that belongs to me! I don't believe it. What a flaming cheek!'

'Well, I think you'll be living rent-free from now on, since Pedro won't be coming back,' said Rico. 'You could always go and live in the farmhouse now, if you wanted to.'

'We've been talking about that. We went up there last week. It was quite strange being there again after all these years. Pedro's left it in a right mess. It's absolutely filthy. It needs fumigating and clearing out completely, for a start. Then it needs a lot of maintenance and redecorating as well. It's going to cost a lot to restore it to a habitable condition. We don't know what to do about it yet,' said Maria.

'Well, there's plenty of time to decide,' said Rico. 'Ana, are there any other unaccounted for transactions in Pedro's account or can we move on to the next person?'

'There are varying amounts between four and five thousand euros being paid into Pedro's account every month and one regular payment each month to Account No. 764111 for one hundred euros.'

'Got him!' said the Inspector gleefully. 'I recognise that number! It belongs to that nasty solicitor I have under house arrest. Now we're really getting somewhere.'

'That wouldn't by any chance be Diego Mendosa, would it?' asked Felix. 'He's the one who swindled my mother by letting Pedro sell land which Mum owned and he didn't. It broke her heart that her own son could do such a nasty thing.'

'Yes, it would, but you haven't heard that from me. I think that Mendosa was probably blackmailing Pedro. Mendosa perhaps recruited him for this lucrative scandal and insisted on a regular payout. It seems to be the way he operates. Proving it is a different matter. Pedro would have known Mendosa though, wouldn't he?'

'I don't know,' said Felix. 'All this unpleasantness with my family happened over twenty-five years ago. I don't know if he has had any contact with him since.'

'It's just that Pedro kept talking about 'The Boss' and his role in the scandal, but he said he had only spoken to him on the phone. He was clearly terrified of him. He was adamant that he had never met him. All he could tell me was that the 'Boss' was male and Spanish-speaking but didn't come from the Islands,' added Rico.

'That would be right,' said Felix. 'Mendosa comes from somewhere near Madrid. He still has a lot of property in Spain and on the Canary Islands as well, I think. It's all rented out. Obviously, he has been investing his ill-gotten gains very wisely.'

'The two factory thugs and the Hotel Manager received regular payments from the same account number as Pedro, but it's not Mendosa's,' said Ana, checking the paperwork spread out in front of her. 'Presumably their wages of sin!'

'Who owns the fish factory as a matter of interest?' asked Maria suddenly.

'It's registered to a Carlos Ramares. It was purchased just over two years ago. Mendosa's firm completed the transaction, but the file has mysteriously gone missing. I was trying to tie Mendosa up with the Professor and the Hotel Manager but there seems to be no connection.'

'Did Mendosa know what the factory was being used for? Is he implicated in this scam?'

'He may well be, Maria, but he is such a lying skunk that I haven't been able to pin him down yet. I've still got his bank statements and lots of other paperwork from his computer to go through and that will take ages.'

'What about their mobile phones?' asked Felix. 'That's how we caught the Professor out initially. Perhaps it would be worth cross-checking the records?'

'Dad, you're brilliant!' said Sandro, erupting with excitement. 'Do you remember all those disgusting lovey-dovey texts on the Professor's mobile which were sent to 'C'? Supposing by a very wild stretch of the imagination that 'C' was 'Carlos' and they were partners in love and crime? Rico, do you still have all the mobiles?'

'Yes, they're back at the station but there was no useful data on them that we could find.'

'Let Sandro have them,' suggested Felix. 'He's a whiz at hacking into mobiles!'

'Okay! It's worth a try. I want to nail everyone involved, if I can. Oh dear! I think I am reverting to the rather unorthodox methods which I heartily condemned only a few weeks ago! I'm very grateful for all your help but this is strictly unofficial or I'll get the sack!'

'Your secret is safe with us, Rico,' said Felix.

'The Professor did spend a lot of time on Lanzarote,' said Ana thoughtfully. 'He never brought any notes back for me to type up and collate, so I assumed he wasn't working. He was always relaxed and happy before he went and he always came back in a foul mood, so perhaps he was meeting a lover there,' continued Ana.

'I can check the dates with Satya and the Security records for you, Rico,' offered Maria.

'That would be very helpful,' agreed the Inspector. 'What a strange person he was!'

'By the way,' continued Ana in a business-like manner. 'There are some very large payments going out of the Professor's account and I have four different destinations.' 'Could they be off-shore tax-free accounts?'

'Yes, indeed they are,' replied Rico. 'He was a very clever operator, but all those funds have already been confiscated by the relevant authorities, I think.'

Rico paused, assimilating the information gathered so far and then suddenly asked Ana:

'How many accounts did you say, Ana?'

'Four different accounts. Two of the accounts were used regularly, the third one occasionally but the fourth one just has two large lump sums deposited in it.'

'Damn it! The Professor declared two accounts and I didn't have the time to double-check. I didn't think it was important as the case wasn't going to court, much to my annoyance and disgust. How careless of me! I criticize my own staff for slipshod work and then I am guilty of it myself! I ought to be shot!'

'Not here, please! It would make an awful mess here in the kitchen and I don't want to be the one clearing it up,' laughed Sandro.

'When did *you* last do any housework, Sandro?' teased Felix, joining in the laughter.

'Just a minute, Rico!' said Ana suddenly. 'I think I recognise one of these off-shore account numbers. Yes! It's the same number that the two thugs, Uncle Pedro and the Hotel Manager were being paid from.'

'Well done, Ana! That's the missing link. Thank you so much. That connects the Professor with the Hotel Manager, Pedro and the two Venezuelan factory thugs and the person who owns that bank account,' agreed Rico. 'I'll contact the Bank tomorrow and find out more details. It could belong to Mendosa, Carlos Ramares or even to someone else we know nothing about yet. I felt certain that there must be someone else in the background manipulating the criminals we have so far identified.'

'He must be a very nasty piece of work if Pedro was so afraid of him,' said Felix.

'Yes, you're right. Quite a tricky customer, I should think. The sooner he's dealt with, the better,' added Rico, thoughtfully.

Suddenly Sandro bounced up from the computer desk.

'Hey, listen to this, guys! I've just checked out the name Carlos Ramares on various websites. One's a politician, one's a folk musician but the third one listed sounds very promising. He seems to be a mega-rich businessman from Venezuela. Widely travelled. Has lived in Africa, India and Dubai. Multi-lingual. Single. No children that he knows of. Likes computer games and cryptic puzzles. Hates sport of any kind. Would like to be a politician one day. Reckons you have to be single-minded to succeed in business and politics,' finished Sandro, enthusiastically.

'Amazing, Sandro! Modern technology, eh! Sounds a fascinating fellow,' said Rico. 'There may, however, be several people of that name and we must not jump to conclusions. It's interesting, though, that he is Venezuelan like our two murderers and has also spent time in India and Africa. Could well be highly significant.'

'Rico, who owns the Clinic in Tenerife? There must be a connection with one of the criminals so far identified,' suggested Felix out of the blue.

'I must be going senile,' said Rico in despair. 'That's the one piece of information I haven't got yet. Something has been niggling at the back of my mind, but I was much too tired to think straight. You're right, Felix. There has to be a connection there for the whole scam to work so well. I'll contact the Land Registry first thing tomorrow and see what I can find out.'

'The Professor rang the Clinic several times, didn't he? I wonder why,' mused Ana. 'It would surely have been in his best interests never to contact the Clinic, wouldn't it?'

'Yes, indeed,' replied Rico. 'If I remember correctly from the print-out you gave me, he called someone there every day for four days in April, but not before that date or after.'

'That's because he usually called them on their mobile,' said Sandro. 'Then their mobile was on the blink or died and they had to use the landline for a while. Same as happened to my friend, Antonio, who works at the Clinic.'

'I don't need a police force with you lot around,' said Rico, laughing. 'You're born detectives!'

'Surely other staff at the Clinic apart from the surgeons must have wondered where all these organs for transplant were coming from so regularly?' asked Ana. 'Is it worth Sandro ringing his friend Antonio to ask if anyone called Carlos worked there? He might even know who owns the Clinic.'

'Excellent idea, Ana. Would you mind, Sandro?'

Sandro duly obliged and they waited quietly while he talked to Antonio. Felix fetched a bottle of wine and five glasses. What an evening!

'Well, there's good news and bad news!' said Sandro, teasing. 'The person who throws his weight around at the Clinic *is* called Carlos and he *is* from South America, but Antonio said his surname is definitely not

Ramares. He said he can't remember it off-hand but he thought it sounded more Indian than Spanish. Antonio will find out for me. He doesn't know if he actually owns the Clinic or is on the Board of Directors or if there is another connection. He isn't there very often, but when he is, everyone jumps to attention. He hasn't been there in the last six weeks or more. Antonio says he's arrogant and suave but everyone is absolutely terrified of him.'

'Wow!' said Felix, handing round the wine-filled glasses. 'The profile fits, even if the name doesn't!'

'Supposing he has a double-barrelled surname and uses one surname for legal transactions and the other for day-to-day business, perhaps to conceal his identity?' suggested Maria, tentatively.

'That's a clever idea, Mum', acknowledged Ana. 'Maybe, he's half Indian and half Venezuelan. That would give a clue as to how he and the Professor know each other.'

'Would you all like a permanent job with the Police Investigation Unit?' asked the Inspector, laughing. 'You don't seem to need my help at all.'

'Of course we do,' countered Sandro, grinning. 'We only provide the brainpower!'

Rico eventually stopped laughing and rummaged in his pockets for some draft documents he hoped he had remembered to bring.

'This is for all of you,' said Rico. 'I'm sorry it's taken so long to organise but the powers that be did eventually sanction my suggestion, I'm pleased to say.'

He handed the papers to Felix, who stared speechless and wide-eyed at their content.

'Are you sure about all this, Rico? It's amazing. I just can't believe it!'

'Come on, Dad,' encouraged Sandro. 'Don't keep us in suspense!'

'It's a natural solution to the problem and won't cause any upset or rumours,' added Rico. 'If you are happy to accept it, the authorities concerned would be very grateful. Without your family's help, this crime would have gone undetected and a lot more people would probably have died. Because it's all hush-hush, they can't officially give you any reward or recognition for what you did.'

'We never expected any,' responded Felix, staring in sheer amazement at the documents.

'This is just incredible,' said Felix. 'This means that the cottage, the minibus, the taxi licence and Pedro's lovely new boat are to be legally registered in our name. That's wonderful, Rico. I can't thank you enough.'

'You're very welcome. I can't thank all of you enough. I'm only sorry that I can't get your inheritance back for you that your brother swindled you out of all those years ago but this will hopefully compensate a little,' said Rico. 'I would also like to treat you all to dinner. Shall we celebrate everything in style on Friday night?'

'Sorry, Rico, we can't do Friday. I've invited Satya, Chano, Domingo and Rafa here for a meal.'

'No problem! Please bring them too, if they would like to come. It will be a pleasure to spend the evening with the whole 'team'. I couldn't have solved this crime without you. You are all invited out to dinner. I want to thank you all for your invaluable help.'

'We need to earn it first!' said Maria, wiping tears from her eyes. 'Is there any other time-consuming paperwork we can help you with? We are more than willing to help.'

'That's a very kind offer, Maria, but I would be breaking every rule in the book if we started work on any other case together. Data protection, confidentiality and all the other useless red tape which plagues us nowadays. As it is, I have broken a few rules already tonight and I feel rather guilty about it, but I am also immensely relieved that the end of this case is in sight.'

'What about us cross-referencing all the mobile records relating to this case, once Sandro has extracted all the data? That would help you and it would really only be a continuation of tonight's work,' suggested Ana playfully.

'That would be great,' admitted Rico, smiling. 'Sandro, would you by any remote chance be interested in joining the police force? You seem to have some extremely useful talents which would benefit us!'

'No way, thank you, Rico. I want to be a pilot, if I can. If I joined the police, I'd probably break too many rules and end up in the cells! I value my freedom,' replied Sandro, grinning happily.

'Well, if you change your mind, you know where I am! Thank you all for a great evening and for all your hard work. I'll book a table for nine o'clock in that new restaurant overlooking the bay and I'll come round earlier with the mobile phones and any records, if I may,' said Rico.

'That'll be fine. We'll look forward to it, Rico. Thank you once again,' added Felix.

After Rico had taken his leave, Ana rang Satya and Felix contacted Rafa, Chano and Domingo. Sandro wandered off to raid the fridge, while Maria sank down on the old leather sofa, totally exhausted by all the events of the last few days.

※

After a two hour wait in the transit lounge under guard at Barajas Airport, Madrid, the Professor had been escorted on to the Boeing 380 which was to take him to Mumbai. This journey seemed endless. Another seven hours flying-time to Dubai, a three hour wait in the transit lounge there and then another three hour flight to his final destination, Mumbai. He was tired and fed up. He was strapped in like a sardine in economy class. He always travelled first class. This was yet another insult he had to endure. Incarceration in various police cells for three weeks followed by house-arrest in some desolate place and then bundled into a police van and taken under guard to the airport in Tenerife to be deported to India. Constant interrogation but he had not revealed anything about his lover, Carlos. Never would he betray him. He had been unable to warn Carlos that the scam had been discovered. Had he been arrested too? Had he been extradited to Venezuela? Six weeks and no contact with his beloved! It was torture. There had been no way of contacting him. He thought on balance that Carlos would escape. He was a very shrewd operator. Oh, how he missed him! Life had been so good! So much money and such great times together!

Then the stupid operations had started going wrong. They suspected that one of the surgeons might be sabotaging them, so that surgeon 'had to return to India urgently', but in fact he was taken to La Gomera and was put in the 'tender care' of the two guards at the factory. They had hoped for better results with the next Indian surgeon. He worked well for a while then he began to complain that the organs for transplant were in exceedingly poor condition and he started asking awkward questions about their origin. So he was transported to the fish factory to operate there so that he could see the origin of the organs at first hand. He hadn't liked that much, reflected the Professor. Carlos had joked about it endlessly and even told him that the surgeon had ended up on a bonfire! As if that were likely! One of the Indian surgeons they had recruited had been doing invaluable research for them for well over a year, but he had to be moved to surgical operations as they were now short-staffed. He didn't appreciate his lucrative contract either. He kept complaining that the donor organs for transplant were incompatible with the designated recipients. What did it matter? You couldn't be too fussy if you needed a new kidney! So a few of the patients had died! So what! Everyone still got paid and the money kept rolling in.

But they couldn't stop the surgeon complaining that it was all unethical and wrong. Then one day, despite all their threats, he refused to operate any more! He just went on strike! How did he dare? Carlos had been furious. So the surgeon was discreetly transferred to the fish factory and made to work there in a much less pleasant environment. These Indian surgeons were so arrogant and ungrateful! They had excellent working conditions in that new Clinic and yet they still found something to moan about. Then six of the Indian transplant patients had become seriously ill. The Clinical Director refused point blank to accept responsibility for the medical complications and had insisted that the gravely ill patients 'convalesce' somewhere else. They didn't want any more inconvenient corpses cluttering up their hygienic environment. There would have been far too many awkward questions and close scrutiny was the last thing they wanted under the circumstances. In desperation, the last six patients with the dodgy transplants had been flown discreetly to La Gomera and installed at the Conference Hotel. He knew that two of the patients had died but he had been assured that any evidence had been erased. The remaining four had stayed on at the hotel for quite a while before eventually returning unobtrusively to Tenerife and on to India, thank goodness. It was such a clever scam! A real money-spinner with benefits all round!

If only they could turn back the clock! They had been so happy in the Canary Islands. Freedom to do what they wanted! It had all worked out exactly as they had planned. He still had no idea why it had suddenly collapsed around their ears. Perhaps Carlos was just lying low for a while until the heat died down? He would surely come and find him and they would quietly set up again somewhere else. With the help of Carlos and his very useful underworld contacts, they would be together again. Carlos would know what to do. Carlos would extricate him from this untenable situation. He only had to wait. Just wait quietly for Carlos. Waiting was, however, very hard and he was not accustomed to the process. It was lonely, exasperating and extremely boring. Life was so empty and meaningless without him. They had never been apart for so long. Where was Carlos? He needed him now more than ever. He could not endure this state of limbo for much longer.

It was driving him insane. How were they going to get together again?

The Indian authorities had informed the Professor that the serious criminal charges against him were in abeyance while the evidence was being cross-referenced and collated ready for prosecution. Meanwhile he would be housed in a small flat in a cheap suburb of Mumbai under constant surveillance. He would never be allowed to leave the country under any circumstances, so no foreign lecture tours. In fact he would only leave the flat itself under escort. He would not be allowed to own a mobile or a computer. He had brought the Indian government into serious disrepute and he was going to be punished for the considerable embarrassment and disgrace he had caused.

Did the authorities really think that he, an eminent professor, was going to put up with that sort of regime? Did they seriously imagine that he would survive with no job, no money, no partner and no fun? Time to work out an alternative strategy.

He had realised to his immense relief that there was in fact no police guard with him on this flight to Dubai. He would be met at Immigration at Mumbai by the Indian police and 'dealt with', so he had been informed. He would have three hours at Dubai airport in the transit lounge. There had to be a way to escape from that, though the area was of course sealed off by Immigration. This would be his one and only chance to escape and he must use it if he ever wanted to see Carlos soon and have a decent life-style. Life would be hell in captivity in Mumbai. No way was he going to endure that sort of existence. No more time for self-pity. The Professor's unprepossessing arrogance asserted itself and added incentive to his thought processes.

'Have you had any more thoughts about the farmhouse, Maria? Would you like to live there or would you rather stay here in the cottage?'

'I don't really want to live there, Felix,' replied Maria. 'Our cottage is small and rather cramped at times, but it's a happy home for us and I'd prefer to stay here. The farmhouse would remind me constantly of Pedro. I can understand if *you* would like to live there but I'd rather not, if that's okay with you.'

'I know it was my childhood home but this cottage is a much happier and more peaceful home and I'd rather stay here, too. So that's settled! What shall we do with the old farmhouse then?' Felix asked.

'What would you think about turning it into flats, when we can afford to do it? Perhaps Rafa would like to take on the farmhouse as a long-term project and do it up over a period of time. He could live there rent-free and eventually act as caretaker/manager for the other flats. It would be much better than where he is living at the moment and he would probably appreciate having company nearby. We do our best but he is still very lonely without Isobel. It would have the additional advantage of keeping him busy and taking his mind off things. Chano and Domingo were talking about the possibility of living here in La Gomera rather than in Tenerife and they might be interested in renting a flat. Perhaps Ana and Sandro would like their own space, too. There are all sorts of possibilities for the future. I don't think our dream of running a business from there is ever going to come to fruition in the present economic climate. At least now we are all using our languages, so part of the dream has been realized. You and Rafa are happy working together on the boat; Sandro wants to be a pilot eventually, but in the short term he is happy to help on the boat and with the taxi service; Ana will go off one day to university full-time or part-time and is very happy working at the Centre for the time being. I shall see how it goes with my new position at the Centre, which will be quite a challenge,' said Maria.

'Let's talk to Rafa tomorrow and see what he thinks. He is extremely good at DIY and refurbishing the farmhouse quietly in his own time might prove a welcome distraction for him. Even though it's over two years since Isobel died, he still finds the evenings very long and empty. It's such a shame they couldn't have any children. You're right. Organising an apartment to his own specifications might give him a new lease of life. I know we all try to include him as much as possible but it is still hard for him without his wife. They tried every possible conventional, homoeopathic and alternative medical treatment but the cancer defeated them in the end. He was absolutely devoted to Isobel. I know how devastated I'd be, if you died, Maria. I'd fall apart, too.'

'I'm not intending to peg it just yet!' responded Maria. 'Let's ask Rafa what he would like to do and we'll go from there. We don't need to decide anything in a hurry.'

Two hours into the long flight and the Professor was quietly congratulating himself on having formulated an escape plan. He still had several contacts amongst the large Indian community in Dubai and hoped he could get in touch with some of them. They should be able to bamboozle the tame officials on duty and get him out of the transit lounge without arousing suspicion if they followed his plan to the letter. He had been carefully chatting up the passenger beside him because he had a very useful laptop and he hoped he would let him use it. He still had a very healthy bank balance under an alias in an account in Dubai. He had been extremely careful not to mention that one to the stupid policemen who were interrogating him. There were, as far as he knew, no extradition treaties between Dubai, Spain and India. In any case, by the time the authorities realised he had not arrived as planned in Mumbai he would have unobtrusively disappeared into Karama, the mixed commercial and residential district in Dubai known affectionately as 'Little India'. He would be quite happy to live in Dubai again. Now for the first step of his bid for freedom. He politely asked the businessman beside him if could borrow his laptop for a few minutes as he wanted to check some arrangements. The amicable passenger agreed without hesitation. Stage one successful! Now to perfect his plan of escape!

'Mum,' said Sandro, teasingly. 'I'm not sure it's good for my image to be dining out with a Police Inspector tonight. I will have no 'street cred' left!'

'I don't think any of your friends are likely to be in that particular restaurant this evening, Sandro, so you needn't worry too much. Of course, if you'd rather stay home and cook for yourself, I'll explain your reservations to Rico. I'm sure he won't mind too much and will accept your reasons.'

'No, no, of course not!' Sandro replied hastily, realising belatedly that his mother had outwitted him yet again.

'I thought you'd be only too pleased to come,' replied Maria, laughing at her son. 'I've never known you refuse a meal yet! I expect your image will recover quite quickly. You never know, it might even enhance it. Your bottomless pit of a stomach will no doubt be extremely grateful that you feel able after all to dine out with all of us!'

'Don't move! There's someone hiding behind that rock over there. I think it's a girl,' whispered Sara's fifteen year old son, Cisco.

'What shall we do?' asked his younger brother, Cesar. 'Can't we just leave her and go back to the camp? I don't want her ruining our adventure. I don't like girls. They're weird. I don't understand them.'

'We can't just leave her. She must be frightened, if she is in hiding,' countered Cisco, trying to rationalise the situation. 'We ought to try to help her, if she is in trouble. She looks half-starved. You work your way round to the right of that rock and I'll go off to the left and we should be able to see if she needs any help. And go quietly, so as not to frighten her any more! Okay?'

The girl remained motionless behind the rock and did not hear the boys moving stealthily towards her. She was obviously terrified when they materialised silently behind her. The fear in her face was, however, replaced by overwhelming relief when she realised that they were just boys and they in turn were almost rooted to the ground in surprise to find a very thin, young African girl in rags. Cisco held out his hand to her in a gesture of help and she accepted gratefully. Using improvised sign language they walked with her back to their makeshift camp where they offered her food and water. She tucked in ravenously to their supplies and thanked them as best she could. She instinctively felt that she was safe with them and knew that they would help her. Cisco realised immediately that she could not spend the night with them, so he quickly called his friend, Sandro, for advice.

'That's an incredibly generous offer, Maria,' said Rafa, as Felix handed round mugs of steaming coffee. 'I would love to do up the farmhouse for you both. It would be a labour of love. I owe you both everything.'

'You don't owe us anything, Rafa,' replied Maria. 'You're part of the family. I know you aren't particularly happy in the tiny flat you rented after you had to sell your house. We don't want to move up to the farmhouse. We're happy here, even if it is a bit cramped at times. It seems sensible to use the farmhouse somehow and turning it into self-contained flats might be the answer. It needs a lot of work and we would pay for all the materials required, of course. Pedro has left it all in the most disgraceful mess.'

'That doesn't surprise me, but I can soon clear up the mess. I really hate where I live now,' admitted Rafa. 'I do love DIY and would enjoy doing up the building in my spare time. I still find the evenings very lonely, as you know, and it would give me something really exciting to do. Thank you both so much. But I insist on paying you rent. I already receive a good salary from our fishing business so I want to pay my way.'

'Well, we'll see about that. If you are doing all the work, we think you ought to live rent-free. We'll discuss all the arrangements in detail later and I'm sure we'll come to an acceptable compromise. The important thing is that you enjoy doing it up and that you are happy there, Rafa,' finished Felix, as Rafa's mobile rang. Recognising Sandro's number, Rafa apologised to his friends for the interruption and then took the call.

Satya went over to Ana's desk and handed her a large white envelope.

'I think you'll be surprised and hopefully delighted when you see what's inside, Ana. This just came in the post for you.'

Ana duly opened the envelope and stared at the contents in total amazement.

'Wow! Awesome! How wonderful! Is it real? I can't accept it,' said Ana in confusion.

'Why not? You deserve it, Ana. Without your persistence Karthik would never have been rescued. He would never have seen his family again. He would not be alive to help so many of his countrymen. It's a generous offer from Karthik and the Indian government. You must accept it,' finished Satya, taking her in his arms.

'It's certainly a marvellous opportunity,' replied Ana. 'But I couldn't go on my own. I couldn't cope. I want to travel but I've never been abroad. I've never even been on a plane. I couldn't do it and I'd miss you terribly, Satya. I couldn't go.'

Satya took out a similar white envelope from his jacket pocket and smiled conspiratorially at her.

'Supposing we went together, Ana? I have been given a ticket too. I would love to show you some of my homeland and I think the Indian government and Karthik would be most upset if we didn't use these airline tickets. Karthik has invited us to stay with his family and Tamarai is dying to meet you and thank you. The Conference Centre can manage without us for two or three weeks. Could you put up with me for a fortnight or so in Chennai?'

'Oh yes, Satya', replied Ana enthusiastically. 'I think I could just about cope with that!'

About an hour later Rafa and Sandro bumped uncomfortably along the dusty forest track in the faithful old truck, following Cisco's surprisingly detailed directions. Eventually they came within sight of the clearing where the boys had been sleeping out under the stars. Cisco and Cesar were delighted and obviously very relieved to see them. Rafa loaded up the boys, their camping stuff and the young African girl and headed slowly and carefully back to Playa de Santiago. Sandro had spoken to her in very broken French and tried to reassure her that she was safe now. He hoped that Rafa would know what to do next, because he didn't! This was far beyond his field of expertise. At that moment his mobile vibrated in his pocket and he extricated it carefully as the truck lurched again alarmingly over the deeply rutted track. He finally managed to read the text and relayed the information to Rafa, who suggested that he ring Rico first and then Satya.

The Inspector was wading methodically through some of the paperwork on his desk when the phone interrupted his chain of thought.

'Hello Rico, it's Sandro. Sorry to interrupt you at work, but I thought you'd like to know straightaway. My friend, Antonio, has just texted me with the information you wanted. The current owner of that posh new Clinic in Tenerife is apparently called Carlos Prabakar. He is a very wealthy businessman. Despite the Indian surname, he comes from Venezuela apparently. I hope that information helps,' finished Sandro excitedly.

'Indeed it does. Thank you very much, Sandro. That's another invaluable piece of the jigsaw. Please thank your friend for me. I look forward to seeing you all later on,' replied Rico cheerfully.

The Inspector put down the phone and allowed himself a quiet moment of triumph.

'Hello Satya, it's Sandro here. We need your help, please. It's urgent. Can you meet us in the car park outside the Conference Centre in about ten minutes? We'll be in Rafa's old truck. I'll explain everything when we see you.'

Sandro returned his mobile phone to his pocket and looked over to Rafa for more instructions. Rafa smiled back and concentrated on reaching their destination with all his passengers and the old truck intact despite the deep ruts and numerous lethal potholes.

'The information from the Land Registry and the bank, Sir, that you requested,' said the young police officer, handing Rico an impressive wad of paperwork.

'Thank you, Manuel. Good work!' The Inspector smiled gratefully at his colleague.

Manuel positively beamed, as he left the Inspector's office, closing the door quietly behind him. Perhaps this Inspector from Barcelona wasn't so bad after all. If you did the job thoroughly, your work was appreciated. That was very reassuring.

In the car park at the Conference Centre Satya was talking quietly and reassuringly to the African girl who had been discovered by Cisco and Cesar. Rafa had remembered Ana telling him once that Satya spoke fluent French so he hoped that he could find out how this young girl had come to La Gomera and why she was obviously so frightened. Sandro hung discreetly around the back of the truck talking to the boys about their latest adventure. Rafa immediately contacted Maria and updated her with events and she promised to come down to the car park as soon as she could. Rafa knew this young African girl had nothing to do with Pedro's lucrative venture. They had only ever 'rescued' young African men, never women, thank goodness.

'Good Heavens!' exclaimed Rico to himself. 'Who would ever have guessed?'

He stared in sheer disbelief at the information from the Land Registry. Mr Ramares had been very busy indeed. So had his partner in crime! He wondered if the Professor had been aware of the connection. On balance, he thought not. Too much jealousy and too much testosterone for such cut-throat business tactics. The information from the bank confirmed what he had suspected and a lot more besides. The phone lines were certainly going to be red hot today. Maria's family would indeed be amazed at how much had been discovered following their amateur detective work. What a train of events unleashed by two very disparate emails!

Meanwhile, back at the Conference Centre, the phone lines had been buzzing too. Maria had contacted her friend and neighbour, Sara, who had kindly agreed to look after the young African girl until other arrangements could be made. Rafa and Sandro had therefore dropped off the boys, their camping equipment and the African girl at Sara's to a warm welcome, before heading back to the harbour to resume work on the boat. Maria had updated Rico on the dramatic turn of events. To her amazement he had accepted the startling revelations remarkably calmly and assured her that he would deal with the problem and make all the necessary arrangements. He would explain everything when he saw them all later on. Meanwhile he would be out of the office for a while on very important business. While Maria was talking to Rico, Satya updated Felix and Ana, who were quite horrified at the latest twist in the tale.

The Inspector had just asked Manuel to accompany him and was about to brief him when there was a timid knock on the door. Rico immediately sensed disaster as his visitor entered. He was not disappointed.

An extremely nervous and shame-faced police officer was standing in front of the Inspector's desk. He had belatedly realised the seriousness of what he had done or rather not done. The Inspector glared at him in cold fury but remained ominously silent as he continued to stutter out his tale of woe.

'I'm very s . . . sorry, Sir. I only I . . . . left him unguarded for t . . . . ten m . . . . minutes while I p . . . . popped out to the sh . . . . shop and b . . . . bought s . . . . something to eat. I n . . . . never th . . . . thought he would t . . . . try to escape. He had n . . . . never tried to es . . . . escape before. In fact, he was a m . . . . model prisoner and I was absolutely st . . . . starving. I . . . I told him I w . . . . wouldn't be long.'

'You did what?' exploded his superior officer in amazement.

'I th . . . . thought he w . . . . was in the ba . . . . bathroom wh . . . . when I got b . . . . back because I could hear the sh . . . . shower running. After half an hour, I got sus . . . . suspicious that he hadn't come d . . . .

downstairs and when I w . . . . went to ch . . . . check there was no-one up . . . . upstairs at all. The sh . . . . shower was st . . . . still running, so I t . . . . turned it off. It was ob . . . . obvious that no-one had had a sh . . . . shower, so I th . . . . thought something f . . . . funny was going on. Then I ch . . . . checked the whole house and the gr . . . . grounds. His car was still there, so he m . . . . must have escaped on f . . . . foot. He couldn't have gone f . . . . far and I didn't know which way he went so I decided the s . . . . sensible thing was to come back here and report, Sir. Then we could organise a p . . . . proper s . . . . search party.'

The Inspector was almost apoplectic with rage at the lame excuses presented to him.

'How could you be so utterly stupid! I gave you a perfectly simple job to do and you have managed to wreck everything. You had instructions not to let the prisoner out of your sight—ever. Yet you did. If you had even bothered to check the prisoner's whereabouts after your expedition to the shop, you could at least have raised the alarm immediately. As it is, you have compounded the misery and he has had almost two hours to make good his escape. The chances of finding him now are very slight. Have you any idea of the seriousness of this situation? He was under house arrest for a very good reason and you have let him escape. You are in total dereliction of your duty. I will deal with your negligence later. Now get out of my sight!'

The unfortunate police officer bolted like a frightened rabbit out of the office. The Inspector explained the situation to Manuel and asked him to put out an immediate urgent alert for the errant solicitor, Diego Mendosa, who had so cunningly evaded house arrest. He didn't think the devious rat could go far without money or passport, but he didn't want to take any chances. Every passenger at the airport and ferry-port on La Gomera and Tenerife was to be checked rigorously. Roadblocks were to be arranged in case he tried to hitch a lift. Mendosa might possibly be armed so he was to be approached with the utmost caution. Manuel rushed off to put the Inspector's instructions into action.

Rico put his head in his hands and almost wept in frustration. How else could this double-crossing swine escape? By private yacht or fishing boat perhaps? He decided to ring Rafa and Felix to alert them to any unusual activity down at the harbour, because it would take at least three quarters of an hour for any officers to reach Playa de Santiago. These damn ravines! They made getting around so difficult and time-consuming unless you happened to be a mountain goat! He organised officers to go down immediately to the harbour and marina at San Sebastian where larger yachts were moored and he requested that the police launches start patrolling the coast as soon as they were able. He warned everyone that Mendosa might possibly be armed and dangerous and could perhaps be with other equally ruthless criminals. Rico hoped he had covered all contingencies. He could not allow Mendosa and his criminal fraternity to escape. Not now. Not ever. Such a scumbag! There was far too much at stake. So near and yet so far! What incompetence! What disgraceful inefficiency! Why was he constantly plagued by the stupidity of the staff? Why couldn't they execute a simple task without stuffing up? Why had they never been trained properly? If only he had realised sooner what was at stake! What a terrible mess!

It was well past five o'clock when Rico finally managed to ring Felix and Rafa. They listened carefully and immediately agreed to help in any way they could. They told him that so far nothing untoward had happened in the last three hours down at the harbour at Playa de Santiago. They also made another suggestion which Rico welcomed and acted upon straightaway. You couldn't beat local knowledge. Rico fervently wished that he had talked to them first. He contacted the police launches immediately and urgently relayed new instructions, warning them again that the criminals were probably armed. It was now almost four hours since that slimy solicitor, Mendosa, had escaped from his secluded villa. Rico realised that he had seriously underestimated his opponent. Mendosa must have had false identity papers, money and another mobile in a safe somewhere in the house. It had not occurred to him to check. In his defence, he had had no idea at that point in time that Mendosa was involved in crimes other than tax evasion and fraud. His contingency plans for escape had obviously been prepared well in advance, should an awkward situation arise. The chances of catching and arresting Mendosa now were diminishing every minute. He debated whether to cancel the celebratory meal that evening. On balance he decided not to. He had done everything within his power. He could do no more. He did not want to be on his own tonight. The officers could ring him if there were any useful developments.

Maria hugged her daughter, as Ana relayed news of her unexpected present.

'You should really have that plane ticket, Mum,' said Ana generously. 'It was you who worked everything out and planned Karthik's rescue. I didn't do anything really.'

'Nonsense, Ana. If you hadn't been so meticulous and efficient checking the emails, we wouldn't have known about Karthik or the scam. You go with Satya to Chennai and have a wonderful time. In any case, I'd never get Dad to India and I wouldn't want to go without him. You really deserve a holiday. You have worked so hard for so long and we are so very proud of you. I'm sure Karthik and his family will make you both very welcome. It will be a fantastic experience. You always wanted to travel and see different parts of the world, didn't you, Ana? Travel is very educational. You need to experience different cultures. Life on this beautiful little island has severe limitations, as you know. Go for it! Just don't do too much lizard-hunting, will you?'

They were both laughing and crying when Sandro arrived home.

It was well after seven o'clock when a rather harassed and tired Rico parked outside the cottage. There was no word yet of Mendosa even though the thorough search of the locality he had ordered was well underway. Rico was seething with frustration at the unnecessary turn of events. He blamed himself for not increasing the surveillance team, but it had never occurred to him that Diego Mendosa, that hypocritical lying skunk, would seriously try to escape. He had erroneously assumed that the solicitor had too much to lose; that he would quietly stay put and ride out the storm, should the police ever be clever enough to obtain any real evidence against him. After all, none of the legal regulatory authorities had ever managed to stop his dubious practices, so Mendosa would have assumed that he was safe from prosecution. Rico had regarded Mendosa as an irritation, as a thorn in his side rather than as a dangerous criminal. Mendosa had played the game well and had lulled him into a false sense of security. He, the seasoned police officer, should have known better. Now he, Inspector Rico Martinez, was paying the price of making such facile assumptions. There was such a complicated web of deceit and intrigue around Mendosa that it was amazing any of it had been unravelled. But Rico had quietly and painstakingly unravelled it, piece by piece. Patiently, he had followed his instincts and reassembled all the seemingly random bits of information and cross-referenced the data. He had solved the crimes, but had let the criminals escape. How incredibly stupid was that?

Sandro had heard a car pull up and had opened the door ready to admit their visitor, Rico. He was looking forward to extracting data from the various mobile phones. He enjoyed that sort of challenge, though he wasn't exactly sure why! When he saw Rico, however, he realised that something was very wrong. He ushered him quickly into the sitting-room where Maria and Ana welcomed him warmly. Rico collapsed gratefully into the proffered armchair and readily accepted coffee and cake. He suddenly realised that he had had very little to eat or drink because of the disastrous developments and he was exhausted. He briefly explained what had happened during the day and why he was rather tired and miserable. Then he handed a bright green plastic carrier bag and a sheet of relevant information to Sandro.

'There you are, Sandro! Six mobiles to hack into and amuse yourself with. Please can you print out any information for me that you manage to extract. These are two of the numbers I am particularly interested in,' said Rico, managing a smile. 'Perhaps one day, Sandro, you would be kind enough to run a training course for some of my officers in the intricacies of hacking into data on mobile phones and computers. I suspect we are going to need such dubious skills more and more in the fight here against crime. You will get well paid for your invaluable tuition. That goes without saying,' continued Rico.

Sandro grinned and accepted the mobiles with alacrity. He went over to the computer desk and happily set to work.

Rico gradually unwound in the cosy cottage environment as he attacked his coffee and home-made cake. He assured Maria that it would not diminish his appetite later on. He was looking forward now to the restaurant meal together. It would take his mind off a disastrous day. It was bound to be a jolly affair with lots of teasing and laughter from all the 'team'. Just what he needed!

Back at the Conference Centre Satya was finishing his call to Jeevan, who promised to bring his colleagues up to speed. The mystery of the temporary occupancy of their research hut in the Garajonay forest had been solved for the time being. The thin young African girl had taken refuge there for a few days. Such strange things seemed to happen on this little island!

Then Satya decided to make a start on clearing the admin papers off his desk and took the paperwork down with the relevant files to the Professor's old office. With a huge sigh of relief he placed them in piles on the large desk ready for Maria on Monday morning. He was so delighted that Maria had accepted the job. He knew it would be rather a daunting task in the beginning but she had such a natural talent for organization and such excellent people skills that she would have the Conference Centre running smoothly and efficiently in no time at all. That would leave him free from stress to develop the various projects which he and his team had decided did merit further research. Ana also wanted to become involved in some of the projects, though lizard-hunting was unsurprisingly not one of them! She was more interested in environmental issues and was happy to leave the rather hazardous lizard surveillance to the others.

Satya was so happy he could have jumped for joy. All his wildest dreams were coming true. Now that the unpredictable Professor had gone, he had the perfect job in a lovely place with a wonderful partner. Later on in the year, once Maria was happily settled in her new role and the team were up to speed with their research, he and Ana would have a fascinating holiday in India. He was looking forward so much so seeing Karthik again and spending time with his family. He was also very excited about showing Ana a little corner of his homeland. He hoped that she would like it. He wanted her to be part of his life for ever.

―――

An exuberant whoop of joy interrupted the conversation in the cottage.

'Are we correct in assuming that you've found something interesting, Sandro?'

'Yes, Rico, I have, but it's definitely not what I expected. The first three phones were very easy to hack and I've got all the data off them. The next two were rather trickier to decipher because their owners had made a better attempt at deleting all the information, even though they hadn't bothered to lock their keypad. The person who owns this last mobile is, however, seriously devious. I read about this technique the other day on the Internet. It's called ID spoofing and it works a treat with my computer. I never ever thought

I'd be using it to solve a crime! I had tried all my usual methods but nothing worked. In desperation I tried this new technique and by pure chance it has given me access to the data. There are some really weird texts, codenames and messages. I'll print it all out for you and then we can cross-reference it.'

'That's marvellous, Sandro. Well done! What would we ever do without you?'

'Sometimes we don't know what to do with him,' interjected Ana, laughing.

'I won't ever have to go to court and give evidence, will I, Rico?' Sandro's delight at his success rapidly turned to anxiety as he suddenly realised what he had done.

'No. Definitely not. No worries on that score.' Rico was quick to reassure Sandro.

'Would you like some chocolate cake, Sandro, to feed your busy brain cells and cheer you up? I know it won't spoil your insatiable appetite.'

'Yes, please, sis,' replied Sandro. 'I think this time I've really earned it!'

Chano and Domingo were already outside the airport building as Rafa drew up in the minibus. They exchanged greetings and climbed cheerfully into their taxi. Rafa updated them on the latest developments as they headed into town and towards the Conference Hotel to pick up Satya.

'I wonder who's behind that particular scam then,' mused Domingo.

'Queer things seem to happen on this beautiful little island,' commented Chano drily.

'Rico was very calm about it all when Maria told him what Satya had found out from the half-starved little girl. It was almost as if he had expected it,' mused Rafa.

'He's a very clever chap, that Rico. I wouldn't want to be on the wrong side of him.'

'He's certainly shaken up the local police force by all accounts,' said Rafa.

'Did it need shaking up, then?'

'Yes, Domingo. It certainly did. Bribery and corruption are unfortunately rife around here. I suppose it's inevitable in such a small community,' replied Rafa with a sigh.

'It's going to be an interesting evening. I'm really looking forward to it,' said Chano.

'It's very kind of Rico to invite us all to dinner at such a posh restaurant. Obviously Police Inspectors are much better paid than pilots!'

'I think he's extremely grateful for what we've done. He's on a mission to rid the area of serious crime. He's a hard-working fellow but also rather lonely, so I hope we all have a good evening together,' added Rafa.

Satya was waiting for them by the main gate, looking very smart in a beige suit.

'You've scrubbed up well,' laughed Domingo. 'You'll put the rest of us to shame.'

'Sorry,' said Satya. 'I didn't really know what to wear. I've never been invited out to dinner before by the police. Had I better go and change into something more casual?'

'We're just teasing you, Satya. Domingo's just jealous because he hasn't got a suit. In fact I'm not sure if he even has another pair of trousers,' said Chano, laughing.

'You look great, Satya. I'm sure Ana will be very impressed,' added Rafa.

'It's not Ana he needs to impress,' joked Chano. 'It's her father.'

The teasing and camaraderie continued as Rafa drove the short distance to their next pick-up point. As the minibus drew up outside the cottage down by the harbour the family spilled out of the front door, preceded by their host for that evening, who appeared cheerful and relaxed. They noisily exchanged greetings as they piled into their taxi. Once his passengers were safely seated Rafa did an accurate three-point turn and headed up the long steep hill to their evening venue.

'This is much more comfortable than that old banger of yours, Rafa,' quipped Sandro. 'There's not much suspension left on your truck, always assuming it ever had any.'

'It's a faithful old vehicle, good suspension or not. It hasn't let me down yet,' said Rafa, smiling, as he reversed the minibus carefully in the restaurant car park.

'I hope it's still legal,' laughed Felix. 'After all, we've got friends in high places now,' he added, grinning at Rico.

Rico joined heartily in the general banter and laughter as they made their way to the table by the huge picture window. Rico had specially requested this table, having admired the view on a previous occasion when he had dined in solitary splendour on his birthday.

'Wow! What a fantastic view!'

'Rico, this is amazing,' added Maria, awestruck by the stunning view of the small town and harbour far below her.

'It's so beautiful,' said Ana, as she stood shyly beside Satya.

'It's like being in the sky, up in the clouds, above everyone and everything,' said Sandro.

'You'd better sit between us, young Sandro, so that we can keep a beady eye on you,' said Chano playfully, as the two pilots sandwiched their young protégé between them. 'We don't want you flying off into the distance before you've learned to navigate. We need to keep your feet well and truly on the ground!'

Amidst the general hilarity and joshing the friends arranged themselves happily around the table and eventually managed to order their choice of food and drink.

The evening was a great success. Rico had not enjoyed himself so much in years. He had worried beforehand that some of his guests would be wary of him and a little reserved but they had all simply accepted him as part of their extended group of friends. Horrendous as the 'Squid Scandal' had been, some good had come out of it. It had brought him into contact with some wonderfully decent people and he felt at home here in this community. His loneliness receded like a bad dream as he realised how much he wanted to stay here among friends whom he respected and appreciated. He had wanted to order champagne to toast the 'team' and their excellent detective work but they had all politely refused and opted for coffee instead. The good-natured banter continued late into the evening. Rico discreetly settled the bill. They all thanked him profusely for a delicious meal and a wonderful evening and suggested that they meet up regularly every month. Rico generously offered to treat them all again but they wouldn't hear of it.

'I have nothing else to spend my money on,' explained Rico. 'I have no social life at all. It's so difficult with this job. Work interferes too much. I'm so glad I have met all of you. I've never had such lovely friends and I can cope with any amount of teasing, as you've probably realised by now! It would be a pleasure to take you all out to a meal again. It would mean a lot to me.'

'That's very kind of you, Rico, but we would never take advantage of you,' said Felix.

'How about a picnic in the forest next time,' suggested Sandro.

'Not with your map-reading skills, Sandro. We'd never ever find our way home,' laughed Chano.

Eventually, still in high spirits, they all made their way out of their splendid venue and settled into the minibus.

'Rico, you haven't tied up all the loose ends for us yet,' prompted Maria.

'What about the African girl?'

'Have you caught up with Carlos yet?'

'Did the bank give you all the information you wanted about the financial transactions?'

'Is Mendosa implicated in any of this?'

'Hey, one at a time! Talk about being bombarded from all sides!'

Rico paused before answering all their pertinent questions.

'I haven't had any news on my mobile tonight, so I can't answer all your questions definitively but I'll tell you as much as I know at the moment. I'm pleased in a way that my mobile didn't interrupt our lovely evening but it means that my officers have not yet located that miserable solicitor, Mendosa, who escaped house arrest today, just as I had managed to put the final pieces in the jigsaw. It's exceedingly frustrating. You'll see why in a moment.'

Rico looked round at his new friends and continued:

'This is all strictly confidential, by the way, and must remain so. I know you all worked out most of the story but I'll just summarise the main points. The idea behind the transplant scam was hatched by the Professor and his lover, Carlos Prabakar Ramares about three years ago. Carlos provided the necessary finance and the Professor provided the academic cover of the Conference Centre to allow the scam to work. There were rather too many people involved to keep the scam foolproof but since most of the other criminals were blackmailed into cooperation, the 'Squid Scandal' would probably have continued undetected for several years, but for your brilliant deductions and intervention. Carlos has made his money by some very dubious business practices but no-one has yet been able to prove indictable criminal activity. He also has a habit of involving himself in projects which provide good publicity and excellent Public Relations status, as for example with the new Clinic in Tenerife. He managed to interest some high profile investors in the scheme and the Clinic miraculously came quickly into being, with incidentally very little financial input from himself. He is an extremely shrewd operator. The Clinic is a great success and the investors are delighted. They would not be quite so delighted if they were to discover what has made them rich and that they, as directors, could be prosecuted. Carlos has not been seen at the Clinic for several weeks now and will probably never go there again. He was tipped off by a mobile phone message from his partner and new lover.'

Rico looked at the surprised faces around him.

'Carlos had in fact two lovers. Neither lover knew about the other. Carlos would meet up in Lanzarote with your wiry Indian Professor in a very expensive hotel suite. My sources tell me that the intervals between each visit were increasing quite considerably, so I am guessing that the relationship was fading somewhat and Carlos was obviously trying to distance himself from the Professor and get closer to the new love in his life. The Professor knew nothing of this. He was obviously deeply in love with Carlos and was prepared to bear all the shame and consequences of the 'Squid Scandal' himself rather than betray him. He is probably waiting patiently in his miserable flat in Mumbai for Carlos to reappear and magic him out of his awful predicament. I'm afraid he will have a very long wait.'

'That's why the Professor was so short-tempered and prickly lately,' commented Satya. 'We couldn't understand it, because the Conference Centre and the Hotel were making so much money for him and yet he was so moody and unbearable.'

Then Rico produced a newspaper cutting with a picture of Carlos Prabakar at the opening ceremony for the Clinic and showed it to the two pilots.

'That's our obnoxious frequent flier we told you about,' said Domingo without any hesitation.

'He was so unbearably arrogant. He just oozed power and control. He made you feel really uncomfortable and inadequate,' added Chano. 'I hated it when he was there.'

'Your instincts were only too accurate,' commented Rico. 'He is a seriously nasty piece of work. He has several identities and is well acquainted with the lowlife of the underworld. We have managed to block some of his bank accounts, which will annoy him, but I suspect he has many others we don't know about and he will pop up somewhere else in the world with another money-making scam if we can't stop him.'

'Why was Carlos able to use the private plane so often?' asked Ana.

'Because he was actually paying for the lease of the charter plane. Fortunately, the Indian government has taken over the leasing arrangements so that the Conference Centre can become a Centre of Excellence as was intended. So our two friendly pilots here will also still be employed, thank goodness. The authorities in Tenerife are also in the process of signing a tourism contract with the Indian government in order to subsidise the cost and run more inter-island flights, so both sides should benefit.'

Just then Rico's mobile rang and he listened intently to the report. The team watched anxiously as Rico's facial expression changed from frustration to relief at the news.

'Yes, definitely. Yes, that sounds feasible. Yes, double-check and let me know. Yes, do it together. Close in on them! And be careful. Yes, do whatever you have to do. I leave it in your capable hands. Good luck.'

'Sorry about that,' said Rico. 'I think the prime suspect just tried hard to bamboozle my officers on the police launch. There is a woman pretending to be asleep in the cabin of that ocean-going yacht which Rafa mentioned. I suspect it is Mendosa in disguise trying to make good his escape. If we can arrest them before they leave our territorial limits, we shall celebrate big time!'

'Who actually owns the yacht?' queried Felix.

'It's registered to a company called CRDM. The two directors of the company are unsurprisingly Carlos Prabakar Ramares and Diego Mendosa.'

'Incredible,' commented Maria. 'Those two criminals are just like squid with their tentacles stretching out in any direction where they can benefit themselves at the expense of innocent victims. The 'Squid Scandal' is aptly named!'

'You'll be pleased to know that the authorities have already suspended three bank accounts belonging to Mendosa and are searching for more. The yacht will also be impounded pending further investigations. I had a very busy afternoon, as you can see,' added Rico.

'Anyway, where was I? Oh, yes. The African girl. A remarkable young lady with great presence of mind. Carlos and his new lover had meanwhile set up another lucrative scam. They were operating a 'high-class' brothel in a refurbished farmhouse near the airport in Lanzarote. Many of the Conference Centre delegates went there on a so-called 'fact-finding mission' apparently. A night out in a brothel abusing very young African girls was the reward for the Americans and Europeans for their generous sponsorship.'

Rico paused in his narrative and looked over to the two pilots.

'It was one of the things you mentioned when we last spoke. I wondered where your delegates went for a night out on Lanzarote. And I wondered why the Indian delegates didn't go there too. They couldn't be visiting any scientific project in the dark, so we questioned the taxi drivers at the airport and discovered the brothel, which is now under surveillance and will be closed down as soon as we have rounded up everyone involved.

The young African girl, Nahla, was destined for the sex-trade along with several of her friends. Someone with an expensive ocean-going yacht has been bringing young African girls into Lanzarote but the engine broke down on this particular trip and the yacht had to put in for emergency repairs at the marina at San Sebastian on La Gomera. Against all the odds Nahla managed to escape from the yacht with the help of one of the marina engineers. The other girls were too petrified to try to escape. Nahla made her way slowly up to the forest for safety and has been living rough for nearly three weeks. She remembered the name of the yacht because she thought it was rather unusual. It was 'Ramadosa'. Need I say more? The engineer confirmed the name and that opened up several new lines of enquiry and led us eventually to the sex-trafficking scandal and the involvement of Carlos and Mendosa.'

Rico paused again to let his audience digest this unpalatable information.

'Poor girl,' said Ana. 'What an awful fate!'

'It was the same African trader who was sending young men to La Gomera for the organ transplant scam for Carlos and the Professor as well as young girls for the brothel scam/sex trade in Lanzarote for Carlos and Mendosa. All the data from the confiscated computers proves the case against them beyond all reasonable doubt and a prosecution should be successful.'

'As you've probably guessed by now, it is the solicitor, Diego Mendosa, who is the new lover of Carlos. While your Professor was fretting away on La Gomera, wondering when he would next see his lover, Carlos and Mendosa were living it up on Gran Canaria, plotting the next scam. Mendosa has done all the legal work and has recruited the staff necessary to run the various enterprises. They are all being blackmailed and are scared out of their wits and are therefore reluctant to say anything about what is going on. The facts are, however, indisputable. It is Diego Mendosa who is Carlos's partner in love and crime. Together this evil combination has made unbelievable amounts of money and in the process they have wrecked the lives of hundreds of innocent people.'

Rico suddenly became aware that they were still in the car park at the restaurant and looked round apologetically at the team. Maria broke the stunned silence.

'I think we need another coffee after all those revelations. Would you take us back to the cottage, please, Rafa?'

After twenty minutes wandering nonchalantly around the transit lounge at Dubai airport, the Professor made his way to the toilets. There were 'Temporarily Closed' and 'Cleaning in Progress' signs outside, but he ignored them and went in. He locked himself in one of the cubicles and he exchanged clothes with the cleaner. This was to be a most undignified escape but he and Carlos would have a good laugh about it afterwards. The Professor reappeared as a cleaner complete with ID badge. He carefully tied up his accomplice and gagged him to make it look realistic and shoved him into one of the cubicles with the suit etc he had been wearing. Picking up the tools of his new trade, the Professor emerged from the toilets, ensured that the signs were still in place and made his way out of the staff exit using the code he had just been given. Mission accomplished! He just had to concentrate on maintaining the subterfuge until he reached the safety of the main exit where a private car should be waiting for him. Now for the high life in Dubai under another identity! There was really nothing money couldn't buy!

The usual noisy traffic chaos in Mumbai! He was now well over an hour and a half late. Hopefully, it wouldn't matter because Immigration would in any case have detained the nasty little academic whom he had been sent to collect and place under house arrest. He had already been on shift for twelve hours and a hot dusty trek to the airport to collect some minor criminal was the last thing he needed. He parked the police car untidily in the taxi-rank near the main entrance and made his way grumpily into the Arrivals area and through to Immigration. Ten minutes later all hell broke loose.